alliancedesign.

Peg Faimon

alliance.design

Uniting Print + Web

design to create a

total brand presence

Dedication

To my children, Anna and Noah, for their inspiration and energy. To my parents, Bob and Marty, for their influence and dedication. And especially to my husband, Don, for his unconditional love, eternal patience, valuable advice and thoughtful support. I love you all.

About the Author

Peg Faimon received a BFA from Indiana University and an MFA from Yale University. She has worked as a designer for corporate and small design firm offices. Faimon is currently a professor of graphic design at Miami University, Oxford, Ohio. In addition to teaching, she maintains a design consultancy. She has received national and international recognition for her design work.

Peg Faimon is also the co-author, with John Weigand, of *The Nature of Design: How the Principles of Design Shape our World—from Graphics and Architecture to Interiors and Products,* also published by HOW Design Books.

Acknowledgments

Writing this book over the last year has been a wonderful adventure. It has given me the opportunity to learn even more about design, branding, technology and the publishing business. Many people along this journey have been insightful guides, thoughtful companions and enthusiastic participants. Thanks to everyone at HOW Design Books for giving me this unique opportunity. Special thanks go to three women at HOW who have shared their knowledge and experience: Clare Warmke, acquisitions editor, for invaluable guidance and expertise; Amy Schell, my project editor, for writing advice and organizational help; and Lisa Buchanan, art director, for thoughtful design advice and for initially connecting me with HOW. Clare Finney, Richard Hunt, Phil Sexton and Christine Polomsky have also been very helpful through specific aspects of this process.

I am also grateful to the fifteen strategic design and marketing firms that have contributed their work to this book, and to their clients for giving permission to have this exceptional work published: Tank Design and ATG, The VIA Group and Inforonics, Kiku Obata and Brown Shoe, Wolff Olins and Rocket, Carbone Smolan Agency and Sesame Workshop, Morris Creative and Hasbro: Tonka, Iconologic and Kilpatrick Stockton, Monigle Associates and TierOne Bank, Landor and Eli Lilly and Company, Zender + Associates and Asbury Online Institute, 300FeetOut and Academy of Friends, VSA Partners and Baker Furniture, Leonhardt:Fitch and RMW Architecture & Interiors, Visual Marketing Associates and Cincinnati Ballet, and SamataMason and MVP.com. There have been many individuals at each firm involved in this contribution. Their assistance has been invaluable and has made my job a pleasure. I learned so much from each person I connected with, either by phone, email or in person. This experience has confirmed for me that the design profession is full of wonderful, generous people.

Thanks to Pamela Fox, dean of the School of Fine Arts, and Jerry Morris, chair of the Department of Art, for granting me a sabbatical from my teaching at Miami University to pursue this project; to my teaching colleagues Tom Effler and Krishna Joshi for doing a great job holding down the "design program fort"; and to Ken Botts, Rondi Tshcopp, Julie Pennington and Derrick Ellis for teaching my classes.

Lastly, and closest to my heart, I am especially thankful to God for His grace and blessings during the last year and to my husband Don, for his encouragement and support throughout this process.

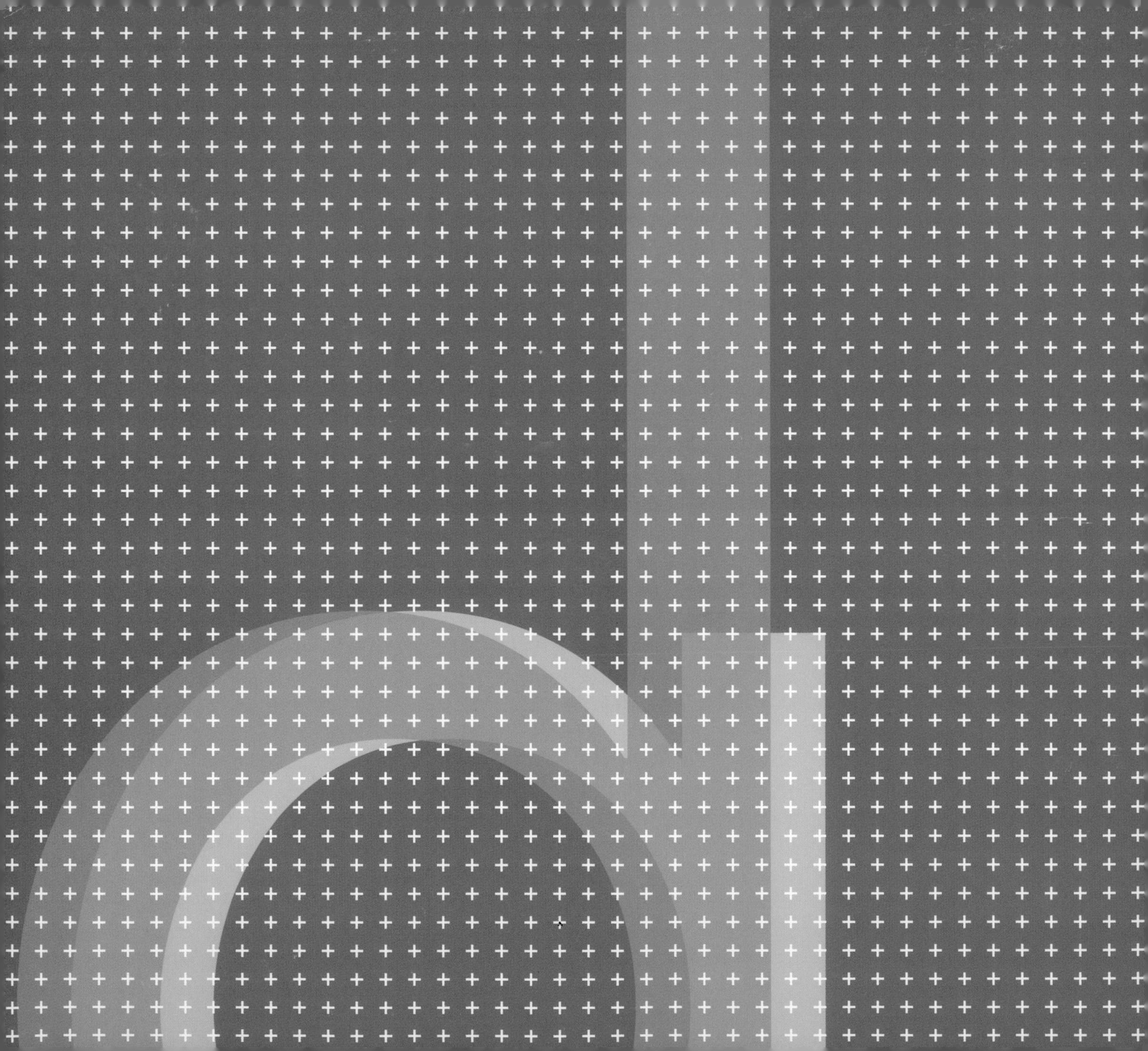

design firms: case studies

design firm highlights

Introduction:

INTEGRATED
brand presence

The last decade has witnessed the evolution of the graphic designer from an end-of-the-process visual problem-solver to an integrated partner in the strategic planning of brand creation and development. Consumers are looking for brands that are relevant, credible, authentic and that connect with them on an emotional level. As we dive into the twenty-first century, with its ever-changing technologies and the challenges of an accelerating daily pace, it is vitally important to humanize brands so they connect on both a personal and global level.

So now designers are called upon to evaluate the visual aspects of a company's identity as well as assess the overall organization, vision and philosophy of a company's communications internally and externally. Design firms must create brands that communicate their personality through a flexible "tool kit" of design elements, consisting of much more than a logo. All of this works together to create a brand experience that differentiates the company from its competitors and interacts with the target audience at multiple touch points. By stressing consistency and integration of traditional and interactive media while creating a heightened awareness of the value of brand identity, the designers can create strong and responsive communication plans.

These developments represent one of the major changes in the graphic design industry and bring a great deal of responsibility and challenge. How do designers best utilize and integrate these tools to the benefit of the client and audience?

This book ventures to answer that question. The top section of this book contains ifteen diverse and enlightening case studies that illustrate ways to bring print, packaging, nvironmental, interactive CD and web design together to combine the best of traditional nd new media. They are categorized according to the industry they come from, but the rocesses each design firm goes through are unique and can be applied to any situation. t the end of each case study is a special spread that showcases the design firm's own dentity collateral.

The bottom section contains useful background and reference material to comple-nent and give context to the case studies. Helpful icons throughout the top pages provide eferences to pertinent information in the bottom pages. The pages are physically split so he reader can access both types of information at the same time but at a different ace...paralleling the nonlinear aspect of the web.

The following pages spotlight the flexibility and evolution of the design industry— he redefining of design. By being immersed in the process and inspirational products of he designers on the following pages, I hope to inspire you to adapt and find new ways to neet the ever-changing technology and business landscapes.

Enjoy!

Tank Design:
ATG

Locations:

Boston, MA

New York, NY

London, UK

Founders:

David Warren

Fred Weaver

Principals:

Ben Segal

Andrew Smiles

Adam Vicinus

Scott Watts

Staff:

Boston: 20

New York: 3

London: 7

20B-23B

 WARREN

 WATTS

 WEAVER

The Firm

David Warren and Fred Weaver wanted to set up a small office where, as Weaver describes, "David and I could work together the way we like to, get some of the bureaucracy out of our hair and hopefully be known in the Boston area as the best design firm in a small community...that age-old story of the small boutique that creates really innovative, creative designs." The result was Tank Design, founded in 1994.

They have since added partners, including Scott Watts, who manages the technical and business issues for Tank, plus they've established offices in London and New York. Weaver continues, "Scott and others bring the interactive expertise we need so we can deliver innovative design solutions through multiple channels, mostly bigger interactive multimedia projects."

The Tank partners speak of their firm's working process as a type of "anti-process." Instead of following a blueprint, every project is very different and requires a unique approach. Although these details dictate variety, their process boils down to a generally consistent four-phase process: discovery and audit, design exploration, design refinement and production. "Design rules for us....We want to keep it about the idea and less about reports, documents and procedures,"notes Warren.

atg ▫

ART TECHNOLOGY GROUP

The Client Project

An excellent example of Tank's approach to design is their client work for ATG (Art Technology Group). Created in 1991, ATG is a leading provider of online customer relationship management (CRM) applications. Warren says, "In a nutshell, their software, their product—ATG Dynamo—and their platform are something that a company could build their web site off of. They deal with the ongoing customer relationship that is driven from all the data that they collect—customized relationships or a customized presentation of information." ATG has an impressive customer base of Fortune 500 companies including American Airlines, Target, J. Crew and General Motors. Although "ATG" is an acronym for Art Technology Group, Inc., the company's full name is rarely used. ATG is simply easier to remember and more effective for visual applications.

The brand manual summarizes: "The ATG brand identity was designed to be unique and easily recognizable, and to communicate our personality on many levels. It conveys our belief that we are authoritative and confident like our position in the market, fast and flexible like ATG Dynamo, and fun, exciting and energetic like the people at ATG."

Tank designed a distinctive logotype that presents ATG and its corresponding "tech mark" in a solid, clear and memorable manner. There is also a family of secondary logos created in a custom font, ATG TheSans. The secondary logos are used on ATG's main product and to differentiate between business groups with the organization on all online and offline communications.

atg**Alliance** ▫
atg **Dynamo** ▫
atg **Global Services** ▫
atg **Innovator** ▫
atg **Insider** ▫

ATG's new logo, top left, is more universal and flexible than their earlier logotype, top right. The secondary logos, above, pull the main identity together with divisions within the company. The consistency of typographic approach brings unity to the system.

11A

ATG TheSans Plain Light
ABCDEFGHIJKLMNOPQRSTUVWXYZ
abcdefghijklmnopqrstuvwxyz
1234567890

ATG TheSans Semi Bold
ABCDEFGHIJKLMNOPQRSTUVWXYZ
abcdefghijklmnopqrstuvwxyz
1234567890

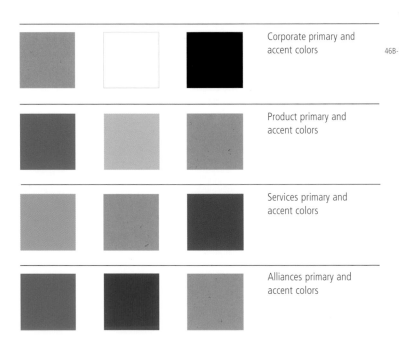

Corporate primary and accent colors

Product primary and accent colors

Services primary and accent colors

Alliances primary and accent colors

The Brand Rules and Tools

Tank developed an all-encompassing two-CD set that includes the important information regarding ATG's brand identity for both on- and off-line work. In order to achieve a consistent voice, the company's graphic assets and imagery must be used appropriately by all who implement and apply the identity. One of the CDs provided to the client includes a library of materials and templates for reference, guidance, inspiration and application.

ATG's own font, ATG TheSans, gives the company's communications a unique and distinctive feel. The typography is straightforward and modern. It's obviously a critical part of the branding package.

According to the brand manual, "A consistent identity is part of our relationship with the public. The more they see the same brand elements used in the same manner, the stronger their recall. If we continue to produce consistently branded, high quality, smart, elegant and eloquent communications, the more confident our prospects and customers will be that ATG is a strong partner now and in the future.'

18B

46B-53B

Imagery is also a very important part of the ATG brand identity. In addition to developing a traditional Pantone palette of primary and accent colors (see left), Tank created a vivid image library consisting of "lightwriting, actual ATG people, and fuzzy people." Each of these categories is color-coded for application: grayscale for corporate literature, blue/green for product literature, orange/red for services literature and blue/pink for alliances. The bold color fosters identification of the business groups within the company.

It's interesting to note that the guidelines and reference tools are also online as an intranet web site. For Tank, these types of guidelines have evolved over the years from a three-ring binder to what they describe as "tool kits." The tool kits give the client a tangible tool for consistently managing the brand, with downloadable imagery and detailed templates and examples.

18B

46B-53B

"The lightwriting represents the journeys we take everyday on the web. Traveling on the web is all about discovery, the unexpected and surprise." – David Warren

ATG Project Team:
David Warren, Design Lead
Ben Segal, Designer
Rob Alexander, Designer
Kelly Heath, Engagement Lead
Linda Koritkoski, Project Management Support

13A

The designs above represent a small sampling of Tank's logo exploration for ATG.

The Process

Tank's design exploration began with the ATG logo, and from there they built the identity's visual vocabulary. The company wanted to change their brand identity to reflect ATG as a corporate entity—much more universal and flexible than Art Technology Group. They also wanted their new logo to be scalable, very large and very small, down to eight pixels. From the beginning, Tank and the leadership of ATG clicked—everything just fell into place. Warren says, "Applying high design to technology was something the client felt was missing in the marketplace. If you look at their competition's collateral and materials, it's as dry as old boots....Our stuff is a breath of fresh air. The culture of the company is so energetic, so enthusiastic, confident and intelligent. They are just not these dry men in gray suits. It's a pretty cool place. The people of ATG are featured as an integral part of the identity to show how essential they are to the culture there. They were photographed as a part of the environment rather than as subjects. We wanted to show them working…real people doing real things."

Over the course of their relationship, Tank has designed some 120 print and interactive pieces for ATG. "Each one meets a different cause," David explains. "This identity and supporting language need to be interpreted by many different groups all over the world. We needed to set up an original system so these different offices, which were sprouting up all over the place, would be able to cost-effectively perpetuate the brand ideas that had been established."

The process for the identity system followed closely to Tank's normal model: Research was 10 percent of the project, design was 80 percent, and the other 10 percent was put into refinement and production.

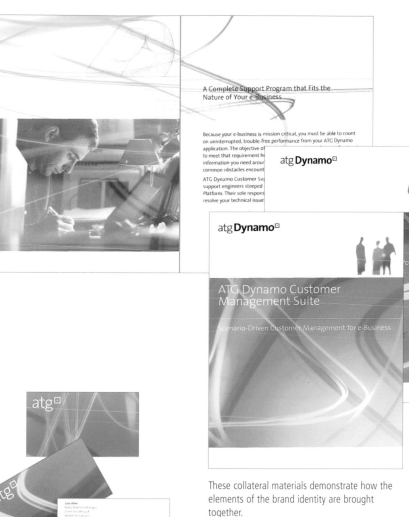

A Complete Support Program that Fits the
Nature of Your e-Business

Because your e-business is mission critical, you must be able to count
on uninterrupted, trouble-free performance from your ATG Dynamo
application. The objective of
to meet that requirement h
information you need arou
common obstacles encount

ATG Dynamo Customer Sup
support engineers steeped
Platform. Their sole respon
resolve your technical issue

atg **Dynamo**

atg **Dynamo**

ATG Dynamo Customer
Management Suite

Scenario-Driven Customer Management for e-Business

These collateral materials demonstrate how the
elements of the brand identity are brought
together.

Multiple-colored business cards bring variety and
allow for personalization.

The Visual Style

The power of holistic branding is
evident in the process and the final ◎ 54B
product for ATG. As the ATG brand
manual states, "Our visual style is
simple and elegant and reflects a
company that is confident, organized, streamlined, purposeful—in
short, an organization that is solid
and easy to do business with. Our
graphics are bold and simple and
do not overwhelm readers with layers of distracting imagery that ham-
per their ability to get to the information they need. This simplicity
allows readers to focus on the content rather than the design."

This annual report spread demonstrates the flexibility of ATG's identity—showing the variety within the system while maintaining unity with other ATG materials.

The Development of Print vs. Web

For Tank, the web is just another medium, another way to communicate the brand to the customer. It's about understanding the channel, the limitations, the audience and its appropriateness, whether it's a web site or a direct mail piece. A web site is as different from an annual report as an annual report is from a brochure. For example, the partners feel that "when you are communicating through an annual report, you have to recognize a different audience, a different amount of content and a different level of seriousness about the content. We think those types of things drive our approach more than whether or not the project is traditional or interactive media. That is something unique to us, although we think more and more the industry is coming to realize that it's all one and the same."

Weaver notes, "The look of the ATG project resulted, in part, from the inherent qualities of the technology used to create it. When we went to design the project, the imagery and the lightwriting look developed the way it did because of the software. Everyone realized that, wow, that's really achieving a lot of the objectives we set out to achieve."

The Ideal Team for Design Today

For Tank, the ideal project team varies with the individual project needs. The lead designers, who have oversight of the projects, decide what is presented to the client and ensure that everything works within the brand guidelines. The individual projects, large or small, are handled by a project manager, and designers are assigned depending on the scope of the project. The designers come from both print and interactive backgrounds but they also employ three-dimensional designers. There's a very diverse mix of design talent in-house. When the need arises and depending on the project, they will partner with out-of-house architects, writers and product designers.

18B

46B-53B

75B

54B

The brand rules and tools intranet web site has all the information necessary to implement the brand identity. With comprehensive digital image files and templates, it's especially helpful to internal employees and vendors.

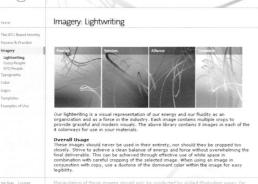

Tank consulted ATG during the creation of design templates for the implementation of ATG's web site. The information is cleanly organized so the company's employees could easily maintain the site.

Innovator is a fun, innovative and somewhat irreverent magazine used as a customer-focused selling tool.

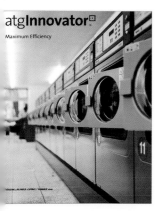

17A

identity

Tank's own identity materials are precise and to the point, with a thoughtful approach. Subtle creativity and contrast between bold, vibrant color and clean white space is characteristic of their work. One of their main promotional materials is a portfolio book that can be easily distributed to prospective clients and interested 38B-42B  parties. It complements their web site.

David Warren
Direct 617 995 4010
dwarren@tankdesign.com

Tank
158 Sidnet Street Cambridge MA 02139
Telephone 617 995 4000
Fax 617 995 4001

www.tankdesign.com

David Warren's simple, clean business card has a twist of personalization.

"Essentially, the overriding philosophy is to strike the appropriate balance between the emotive and the rational."
– David Warren

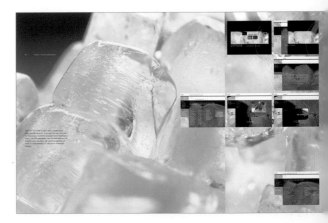

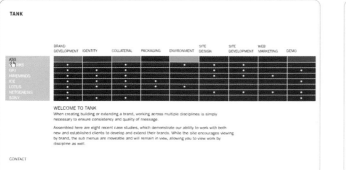

Tank's web site is well-organized, and the information about their work and clients is easily accessible. However, there's also an element of play: you are introduced to the site with a simple yet mesmerizing animation of pulsating rectangles; roll-overs in bright colors add interest and variety; and floating navigational boxes allow the viewer to organize the page and add a greater element of interaction.

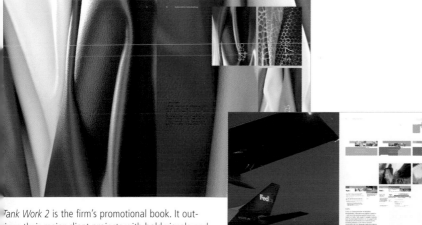

Tank Work 2 is the firm's promotional book. It outlines their major client projects with bold visuals and clear, concise text. Sample spreads shown left, above and right.

The VIA Group

Inforonics

Locations:

Portland, ME

Columbus, OH

Boston, MA

New York, NY

Founding Partners:

John Coleman

Rich Rico

Principals:

Maria Chambers

Ken Dec

Peter Greer

Dave Jackson

Leslie Kaplan

Sara Morris

Greg Smith

Peter Troast

Staff:

100 professionals

BULL

The Firm

What's in a name? When you're talking about The VIA Group, a lot. VIA stands for Vision, Instinct and Action. Founded in 1993 by Rich Rico, in Columbus, Ohio, and John Coleman, in Portland, Maine, they've added Boston and New York offices and have grown to over 100 professionals focusing on four areas: strategy, communications, design and technology. "VIA seeks to balance technical knowledge and strategic direction with instinct and creativity," says Rico. "What we do is focus on audience-based research that affects everything we do. How we say it, how we write it, how we design it and how it's branded from a positioning standpoint and then how it's distributed and disseminated."

What makes them different? Rico continues, "Everyone across all four disciplines—strategy, technology, design and communication—gets involved in the primary research, and that infuses them with an understanding that they can't get from a research report." With this philosophy, VIA creates award-winning solutions and rich brand experiences for a notable list of national and international clients.

VIA's size is an asset. They feel they are small enough to maintain truly integrated communications yet large enough to offer a wide variety of capabilities. "Many design firms don't have writers, communications, media or planning teams, so they outsource to a freelance person that might not know a lot about the strategy. We have all of those links in-house," explains Design Director David Bull.

69B

54B

inforonics

The Client Project

An excellent example of VIA's holistic approach to building, positioning and promoting the brand is their work for Inforonics. Headquartered in Littleton, Massachusetts, for almost forty years, Inforonics has developed complex data management solutions. Despite their long history in the field, Inforonics had very little brand recognition in the marketplace. Although they were committed to rapid change and staying ahead of the technological curve, they needed a brand identity that effectively communicated that promise.

Following the initial discovery phase, VIA's analysis demonstrated a need for a new strategy and brand identity, complemented by the history and tradition of the name. They developed a focused and descriptive list of strategic, audience-based positioning themes. Their audience should be: deep creative thinkers, information experts, state-of-the-art technologists, relationship-driven partners who are sensitive to client needs, business builders and proactive change agents who are quick, agile and trustworthy. Their positioning statement grew out of these attributes: "Inforonics builds, hosts and supports complete Internet solutions for companies looking to capitalize on change."

The identity guidelines describe the resulting logo: "The Inforonics identifier is a hybrid of a monogram and a symbol. The *i* is comprised of a series of dots on a grid, creating clarity out of chaos. This *i* is based on the Courier typeface, which is associated with information processing and software coding."

When the Inforonics identifier and logotype are used together, above, they create a strong signature for the company. The identifier and logotype also appear separately in an environment supported by the other visual elements of the Inforonics identity (see next page).

Earlier Inforonics logos, below.

Officina Book Serif
ABCDEFGHIJKLMNOPQRSTUVWXYZ
abcdefghijklmnopqrstuvwxyz
1234567890

Officina Book Sans
ABCDEFGHIJKLMNOPQRSTUVWXYZ
abcdefghijklmnopqrstuvwxyz
1234567890

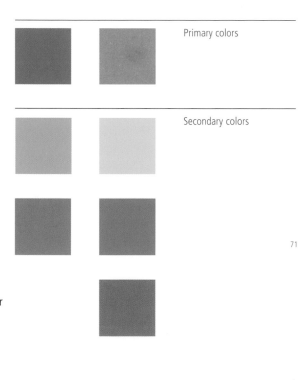

Primary colors

Secondary colors

Inforonics Project Team:
David Bull, Design Director
Allen Dudek, Information Architect
Oscar Fernández, Design Director
Jennifer Juan, Designer
Laura Keen, Writer
Jennifer Keller, Account Manager
Keith Novicki, Senior Designer
Shelly Pomponio, Production Manager
Rich Rico, CCO, Founding Partner
Jeff Tremaine, Lead Strategist
Wendie Wulff, Senior Practitioner

The Brand Rules and Tools

As the Inforonics identity guidelines conclude: "Following these guidelines will help establish the Inforonics identity. Establishing the Inforonics identity will strengthen market presence, build consumer confidence and help consumers select Inforonics products and services."

The guidelines are flexible, unlike the standards manuals of the past. Bull describes VIA's intent: "It is not a strait-jacket. We purposely use friendly language. We don't just show the visual elements but we talk about our thinking and why it's appropriate. In developing anything, we use this gauge of appropriateness from our research to the audience. We're not trying to have one certain look or style, because 71B every audience is different. We certainly are familiar with past classic cases, but we don't look to those types of things for inspiration. We feel that since we are research based, we can grow something new and appropriate out of that content and research. We are not recycling anything and we are not prescribing any one

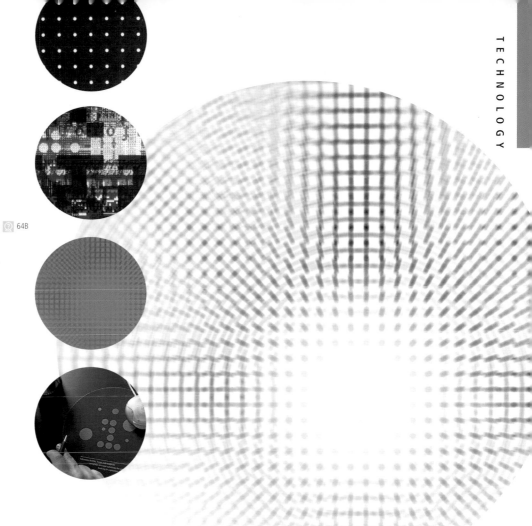

visual language or approach—that's uniqueness. That is really what a brand is. It is the differentiation between you and your competitor that we're after."

64B

In addition to typographic and color guidelines, VIA created a wonderful palette of textures that add variety and depth to the design work. The patterns are an interpretation of the dots within the identifier itself.

The use of circular forms is integrated into other design details like the cropping of photographs, the rounded die-cut corners on the stationery and the round address window on the envelopes. Even the mouse pads are round.

Inforonics is down to earth and has a humanistic approach.
Even the lowercase used in the logo
and the softer roundness of the dots
communicate friendliness and approachability."
– David Bull

23A

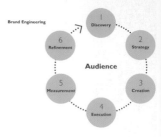

Above are various directions in VIA's design exploration of the Inforonics logo. David Bull explains, "We do many iterations and don't get drilled into one direction. We try to work abstractly, because the more literal you get, the more limiting the design solution."

The Process

20B-23B As the VIA web site explains, "The VIA brand engineering process focuses our strategic vision and creative instinct, putting them into action for clients. It is highly disciplined: grounded in research, organized in discrete steps, executed with clear deliverables, designed to achieve results. The collaboration of diverse disciplines in VIA's methodology creates an environment in which multidimensional brand solutions are born. Not limited to any one communication method to solve clients' problems, this team is relentless in its pursuit of solutions with bottom-line impact."

The Inforonics project is a classic example of the VIA process. Bull and his team remember the initial meeting with the client: "They threw the business card in front of us and said, 'What do you think?' That was their opening statement. Everybody at the table had to say what they thought—brutal honesty." As the project developed, the VIA team worked closely with the color palette. Originally everyone used aggressive, hot colors, but eventually they decided to stay with a refinement of the company's established corporate color, purple. VIA felt the choice helped differentiate Inforonics in the marketplace. The combination of purple and gray as the primary palette is also very cost effective. The secondary palette is used when cost allows, and it adds flexibility to the system.

25B Strategy was extremely important in the development of the Inforonics project. In the beginning, no one, including the CEO, could concisely and distinctly state what the company was about. A key challenge presented to VIA was the development of this important positioning statement, which could be boiled down to a single sentence. At the launch party each employee was given a brochure that presented the statement, the brand attributes, the tagline and the logo. It was something the employees could have right in front of them to help them understand and internalize the brand.

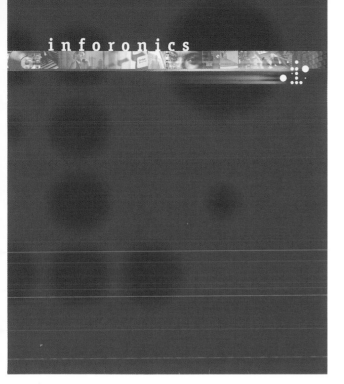

The Implementation

The execution of Inforonics' brand identity is a clear reflection of the company it symbolizes. Every application communicates a message of quality to the employees as well as the customers. Bull summarizes, "It was great to see a company really into the brand. They were very excited about the process and implementing it. That was a great thing for VIA."

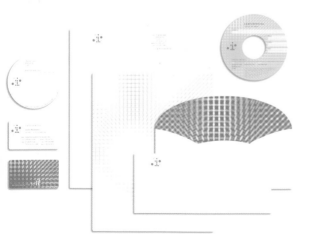

The business papers for Inforonics are a wonderful example of variety within unity. The visual language background elements (patterns, die cuts and type) are composed in a manner that reinforces a total brand personality.

25A

The Color Palette

Due to the friendly corporate personality of Inforonics, VIA wanted to communicate a sub-dued, softer approach than the competitors who were primarily using intense acidic colors. Matching the voice tonality to the visual tonality was very important, and the colors had to be right. The primary color for the brand is Pantone 667, a very specific purple. The fact that all of the major materials for the brand launch were two color meant that getting the right purple was a big deal. VIA ran into some software calibration problems and web-safe color issues. The colors weren't initially consistent, so refinement was especially important.

Generating excitement among the Inforonics employees was an important element of VIA's strategy. One method was to create fun and playful giveaway items. This also demonstrated the consistency of the implementation, even down to putting the logo on a purple sucker.

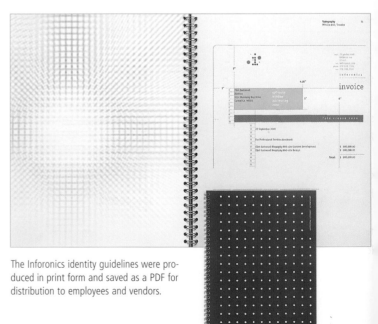

The Inforonics identity guidelines were pro-duced in print form and saved as a PDF for distribution to employees and vendors.

D E S I G N   T I P
VIA uses the semantic differential, a research device, to analyze and refine logo ideas. Here's how it works: Key word attributes are developed and placed on one side of a chart. Words with the opposite meaning are placed on the other side. Consumers are shown mark concepts by VIA researchers, and the respondent is asked to select the words that best describe the mark. They also scale the degree to which the words describe the mark.

Primary and secondary pages for the Inforonics new business generation web sitelet.

The Web Sitelet

An opt-in e-mail web sitelet was a key piece of the strategy for new business generation. Targeted at four audiences—strategic consultants (without technology capabilities), advertising PR firms, manufacturers and other IT consultants—the sitelet was distributed through an e-mail list. Those solicited could click on a link that took them to a home page tailored specifically to them. Going one step further, they arrive at the sitelet, which detailed all the Inforonics capabilities.

Each of the six sections was color-coded for ease of use. This color coding appears on the left side bar, as well as in the drop-down menu at the bottom of the page. Each headline also corresponds to the section color.

The overall shape of the page, with rounded corners, echoes many of the applications. The use of color, typography and white space also link this interactive piece with the look and feel of the print materials.

27A

identity

The Latin meaning for via, "the way," aptly illustrates how VIA guides its clients to success, and VIA's identity materials clearly communicate this vision, instinct and action. There is a strong balance between the rational (clean and well organized) and the emotional (bold and playful), which complements the firm's philosophy.

38B-42B

Be curious

Honor the process

Think like the audience

Create respect

Be on time

Be on budget

Figure it out

Find the magic

Do work that makes you proud

Believe

— www.vianow.com

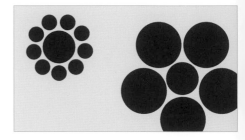

The firm stationery, above, and folder, on the opposite page, are key communications vehicles. At VIA, each employee creates a design for the back of their own business card, right. Allowing for personalization, this gives each professional a sense of individuality within the larger whole of the company.

VIA's web site is a wealth of information. Two key content features are the process section, which outlines VIA's unique approach and vision and the white papers section, which features an in-depth look at the philosophy and thinking behind the company's founders and employees. Visually, the site is well-organized and clearly designed. The images in the lower left section change periodically to add movement and interest to the page.

In such applications as the pocket folder, left, and a case study summary, right, consistent use of the logo and color treatments link the materials into one cohesive package.

The Approach: Put forth a vision, follow through with details

Kiku Obata

Brown Shoe

Location:
St. Louis, MO

Principals:
Kiku Obata
Kevin Flynn

Staff:
30 professionals

The Firm

Kiku Obata has been around architecture her whole life. At the beginning of her career, she worked at HOK, her father's prominent architecture firm. In 1977, she and another designer, Kerry Kuehner, left HOK to strike out on their own. Kiku explains, "At first the firm concentrated on graphic design and environmental graphics. At that time there weren't many firms doing three-dimensional work. My goal was to be able to do all kinds of fun projects. I've always been interested in retail and general communication to consumers, so that is really the focus of the firm. Everything we do is based on a strong idea that meets the clients' needs and communicates with our clients' customers. We feel very strongly that everything we do should make those connections and have some way of emotionally resonating with our clients and their consumers or customers." Kevin Flynn, Obata's current partner, is an architect who brings a wonderful interdisciplinary mix to the leadership.

54B

Currently, the firm has approximately thirty employees. The firm has graphic, interior, industrial, environmental, lighting and architectural designers. "We have a very disciplined process to make sure everyone is successfully integrated," Obata says. "At thirty, we can pay attention to the detail of what we are designing and also pay attention to our staff and our clients."

Teamwork is very important at Kiku Obata. A team leader is chosen from any of the disciplines based on the needs of the project. There will also be representatives from other disciplines. Employees may work on the team, or they may act as consultants, bringing ideas to the table.

Old Brown Group logo, above, and the new Brown Shoe logo, right.

BROWN SHOE®

The Client Project

The Brown Shoe web site tells the story: "More than 120 years ago in 1878, a young man named George Warren Brown believed St. Louis could become a manufacturing center for the shoe industry. He invested his life savings and founded his own little company to manufacture and sell shoes." Today, Brown Shoe is the number-one retailer of value-priced, brand-name shoes for the whole family. Brands such as Famous Footwear, Naturalizer, Dr. Scholl's and Buster Brown come under the Brown Shoe umbrella.

Brown Shoe diversified in the 1970's and changed its name to Brown Group. During the seventies, eighties and early nineties the company lost the strength of their identity and their market share. At that point they decided to return to their roots, the shoe industry and their previous name. Obata explains, "They hired us to create a new brand identity program, and we recommended that they simplify to Brown Shoe. It was very concise and very clean."

The new logo is an abstract representation of both a *B* and a pair of shoes. The simple and clean design suggests a footwear company "on the move" and represents Brown Shoe's mission to be "The Leader in Footwear." The comprehensive strategic brand identity program consisted of a new logo, brand rollout materials, a brand "voice," street banners, T-shirts, corporate trade ads, temporary signage, stationery, forms, brochures, publications, corporate and event signage, a graphic standards guide and a new web site.

38B-42B

31A

News Gothic
ABCDEFGHIJKLMNOPQRSTUVWXYZ
abcdefghijklmnopqrstuvwxyz
1234567890

Bembo
ABCDEFGHIJKLMNOPQRSTUVWXYZ
abcdefghijklmnopqrstuvwxyz
1234567890

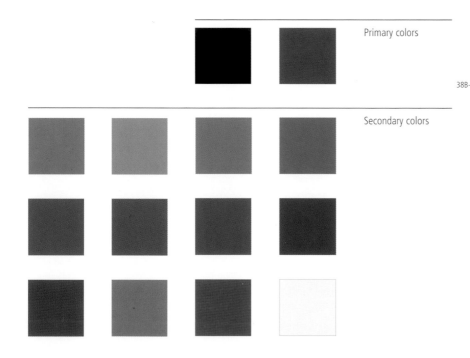

Primary colors

Secondary colors

38B-42B

The Brand Rules and Tools

The identity guide describes the brand's mission: "At Brown Shoe, we want the world to know we're a leader, we're a lifestyle, we're dynamic and we're excellence in execution. We work hard to keep our consumers looking good and feeling good. In turn, we are mindful of our own image as an industry leader and work hard to present a recognizable and unified identity."

The colors chosen to represent Brown Shoe communicate a strong, solid presence and classical feel. The primary colors are used in the logo. The secondary colors are meant to enhance the tone and content of all Brown Shoe communications. There is also a softer, lighter palette of greens, tans and yellows that is used as a support palette when lighter values are more appropriate. The colors are often implemented throughout the graphics in a grid pattern.

Type also reinforces and expresses the company's personality and identity. Two type families, Bembo and News

Brown Shoe Project Team:
Kiku Obata
Scott Gericke
Amy Knopf
Joe Floresca
Jennifer Baldwin
Teresa Norton-Young
Carole Jerome

Gregg Goldman, Photographer
Gen Obata, Photographer

Gothic, were chosen for their precise, straightforward, easy-to-read style. These are the preferred typefaces for external communications. Kiku Obata understood that not all computers within the company would have these typefaces, so for internal communications and word processing they also selected two complementary faces which are readily available on Macs and PCs.

Another important aspect of the brand identity are words, see right. The word *Be* is a call to action. By selecting a few well-chosen words and linking them to *Be* the essence and spirit of the brand is communicated—"Be Smart, Be Creative. Be You."

"To manage a brand you must make sure you always touch base with who you are as a company, your capabilities and your credibility with your audience."
—Kiku Obata

Be Smart
Be Creative
Be Together
Be Cool
Be Real
Be Dynamic
Be Innovative
Be Successful
Be Competitive
Be Exciting
Be Impressed
Be Committed
Be Versatile
Be Sensitive
Be Focused
Be You.

33A

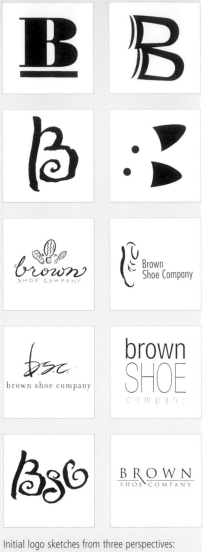

Initial logo sketches from three perspectives:
B, full company name, and initials

The Process

20B-23B Obata defines the firm's process: "I feel my role in the firm is to set the vision for the company's projects—not all projects, but most projects—and then help in terms of designing strategy and ideas with the teams. It's really sort of a collaborative effort. The design team runs with design and implementation and I touch base with them on that. The team size can vary from two to ten, depending on the project size and scope. Most of our work is ongoing and we work for clients on a regular basis."

The team worked closely with Brown Shoe's new chairman, Ron Fromm, who recognized the need for a new identity. KO & Co. came in and conducted research about the company, and interviewed thirty or forty people in management and different divisions. They wanted to understand their work, challenges and internal feelings about the company. One of the rallying cries from the chairman had been, "One integrated company." KO & Co. set out to help the whole company understand the shoemaking process, from conception to the foot of the consumer.

The other big realization for the company was that they weren't a manufacturing company anymore. They were really a fashion company and needed to communicate that point. KO & Co. also compiled a list of all of the brands that Brown Shoe is responsible for and compared it to competitors. They discovered that Brown Shoe makes more shoes than anyone in the world, so they coined the phrase, "The leader in footwear." As Obata describes, "It was really a point of departure for them to say, "Here is who we are today, we are this fashion company and we are pretty cool, let's go for it."

Be Fun.

BROWN SHOE

The Implementation

As the brand manual describes, "Every means of expression sends a message. Our communications materials reveal the spirit and personality of our company. We use high-quality, environmentally friendly paper stocks. Our design formats afford optimum legibility while reflecting a consistent look....At Brown Shoe we epitomize excellence in execution."

Be You.

Various print materials include ads, stationery, promotional brochures, specification sheets and promotional shoe box.

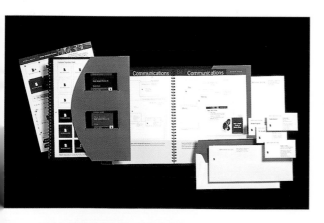

35A

Multi-Dimensional Applications

38B-42B Before the rollout of the new brand identity, the perception of Brown Shoe was that they were a leader in the industry but not necessarily a fashion leader. With only eight to ten

18B weeks to transform the image of the company, KO & Co. relied heavily on the great relationship they built with the client. Immediately following the logo design and brand rollout kit, the three-dimensional applications of signage and environmental graphics helped trans-

46B-55B form the company's surroundings. Following that, additional materials were rolled out, including print materials and the web site. Through this strong series of consistent images in a short span of time, the brand was established. The multi-dimensional nature of the work helped to holistically communicate the new brand throughout the company's internal environment, as well as externally to the public.

A wide variety of print and three-dimensional applications, like signage, banners and T-shirts, help to spread the word about Brown Shoe's new brand identity.

The web site template, above, developed by Kiku Obata & Company. Other pages, right, were developed by the Brown Shoe in-house team using the template.

73B

The Web Site

Once the brand identity was established, KO & Co. worked very quickly with an internal Brown Shoe team to set up a series of templates and design guidelines for the web site. Their in-house dedicated team adds content to the site consistently and ensures that the guidelines are maintained.

Obata talks about how KO & Co. works with their clients: "If we are doing a web site, it is in conjunction with a brand. We've found that most of the bigger clients we work with have an in-house capability to do all of the programming and development, so what we bring to the table are the ideas, aesthetics, functionality and architecture of the web site. We usually team with the client, which I think works great. It makes the transition to their ongoing maintenance of the site much easier because they build it."

75B

identity

KO & Co.'s own identity is crisp and bold. The strong use of the circular element within their applications is softened and complemented by the shadow element. The consistency of the materials reflects the confidence and clarity of the company's vision.

38B-42B

The folder, stationery and labels work together to give the company a holistic appearance and a great first impression.

KO & Co.'s web site is clear and easy to use. Splash page animation reveals specific information about their capabilities and mission, and adds interest and variety to the site.

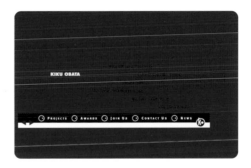

Consistency is maintained, even down to the zip disk covers.

We spin concepts,
weave strategies
and entwine imagination.
— www.kikuobata.com

Wolff Olins

Rocket

Locations:

London, UK

New York, NY

San Francisco, CA

Tokyo, JAPAN

Madrid, SPAIN

Lisbon, PORTUGAL

Principals:

Brian Boylan

Charles Wright

John Williamson

Kate Manasian

Robbie Laughton

Eric Scott

Staff:

150 professionals

The Firm

A world leader in the field of branding for close to forty years, Wolff Olins provides its clients with unique and powerful ideas. With clients such as the Athens 2004 Olympic Committee, Credit Suisse, Orange, Tate and the World Gold Council, Wolff Olins has created worldwide brands. Michael Wolff and Wally Olins joined together in the mid-1960s to create a design company that didn't just focus on looks but on ideas. The company expressed an optimistic belief that there was "always a new way, a better way" of doing something. During the 1970s and 1980s they became more concerned with the consistency of identity. By the mid-1990s they further developed their focus to a brand consultancy. The brand idea became central to their philosophy. They discovered that "people don't want to just buy a product, they want to buy into an idea."

As described on their web site, Wolff Olins' philosophy focuses on this pursuit of the idea: "A big idea has to be *radical*: conveying a sense that things can be done in a new way, that the world can be changed. It has to be *social*: appealing to the hearts and minds of people, it has to have been seen to be true and relevant. Finally it has to be *tangible*: detectable in everything an organization does—in its communications, behavior and products."

Creative Director Robbie Laughton describes the company culture: "There is a sense of belonging to something that is greater than the sum of its parts. It's a very rewarding place to work."

47B

®rocket

The Client Project

Wolff Olins prides itself on being local as well as global. Laughton elaborates, "Every client is different, even if they are from the same sector or from the same country." This individualized treatment is clearly evident in Wolff Olins' work for Unilever's Rocket. As their project case study states: "In September 2000, Unilever approached Wolff Olins with a plan to revolutionize the way people eat when they get home from work. Their idea was to provide commuters with freshly prepared ingredients that they could pick up at the train station, take home and turn into a great meal in just ten minutes."

Unilever had an interest in new initiatives—looking at certain markets and future trends and coming up with something new that people would really want. Rocket was such a new venture. Simon Clarke and Owen Johns from Unilever came to Wolff Olins because of their strong track record in creating and developing brands. Initially, they didn't want to see any specific credentials, and they didn't speak about the project details. Laughton describes the first meeting: "They wanted to get to know our attitudes. On that particular day I wasn't very well dressed, really scruffy, and the other creative director, Lee Coomber, was very smartly dressed. There was a big contrast and I think that really worked in our favor. Our characters were rather exaggerated." From that meeting the Wolff Olins team went on to a briefing session about the product, which sold them on its unique benefits and its ability to deliver on its promise.

The primary mark, top.
The take-away packaging in the form of an insulated silver bag, above, is intended to mimic the consumer's fridge at home. This reinforces the idea that going home is an attractive alternative to eating out.

41A

Linotype Univers Light
ABCDEFGHIJKLMNOPQRSTUVWXYZ
abcdefghijklmnopqrstuvwxyz
1234567890

Linotype Univers Bold
ABCDEFGHIJKLMNOPQRSTUVWXYZ
abcdefghijklmnopqrstuvwxyz
1234567890

Primary colors

Real life, Beautiful food

The Brand Rules and Tools

Laughton describes WO's implementation of brand guidelines: "Brands change, companies change, and therefore we want to keep it flexible, so you can use elements from it. We've partnered with wonderful agencies, and the best way of working with them is to set them free, not constrain them. You do need consistency—the same tone of voice—but we also need to give these agencies the right to do creative work."

The brand tool kit for Rocket is clear and straightforward, like the product. "The name was chosen because it takes the consumer on a journey between real life and beautiful food. It also conveys the speed of the product and suggests modern ingredients that will be found inside." Linotype Univers is used throughout Rocket's identity. Its clarity works well in print and interactive applications and complements the logotype.

Rocket Project Team:

Mike Jefferies, Account Director

Robbie Laughton, Creative Director

Lee Coomber, Creative Director

Dave Linsley, Interactive Consultant

Daniel Letts, Interactive Producer

Helena Gibbins, Producer

Samantha Zak, Account Administrator

Simon Clarke, Designer

Sam Wilson, Designer

Paul Shreiver, Implementation Designer

Jenie De'Ath, Design Specialist

Caroline Schroder, 3-D Designer

Zoe Fugler, 3-D Designer

The color palette is limited to three colors. Green, silver and white work together to communicate the freshness of not only the product but the concept behind the product.

Photography also plays a key role in the brand tool kit. Enlarged and cropped images of floating fruits and vegetables suggest planets, reinforcing the space metaphor and strengthening the visual communication of the applications.

43A

The Process

Working closely with the client, the Wolff Olins team began by fully researching the product. They attended demonstrations by a leading chef and soon realized that the product easily fulfilled its promise of fresh-cooked, restaurant-quality food in just ten minutes. Three approaches were investigated: "The first approach used one of Unilever's existing brands, Knorr, to establish whether or not this could do justice to the product. The second utilized a descriptive approach, relaying the benefits of the product, clearly and simply. The third worked by acknowledging the real-life situation of the target market and promising to take them on a journey to discover beautiful food. The third approach was chosen as the final: with real life at the start of the journey and beautiful food as the destination, the product was positioned as the link between the two."

20B-23B

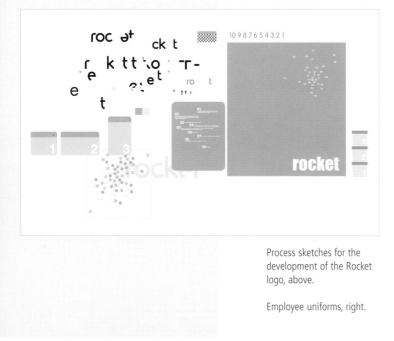

Process sketches for the development of the Rocket logo, above.

Employee uniforms, right.

The Launch Stations

Once the brand concept and name had been established, Wolff Olins set out to apply it to the retail environment. "The Rocket kiosk is designed to be the launch pad where you start your journey to beautiful food. It deliberately puts the food on display, like a fridge, to help speed the choice for the consumer."

Launch stations during business hours, above, while closed, right, and refrigeration display, top.

45A

The Life Beyond Fast Food

Wolff Olins developed the brand idea of "Real life, Beautiful food" by linking it with "going home," positioning it as a valid lifestyle choice to going out or staying late at the office. Going home becomes the new cool thing to do. The visuals support this theme. The color, typography and photography communicate a modern, playful approach. Laughton elaborates, "It doesn't happen that often with clients that they completely trust you with everything. This is one of the most exciting jobs I've worked on, by far."

Menu, above; subway signage, top right; and packaging, bottom right. All combine to create a consistent and pleasurable experience.

The web site allows consumers to order their selections online so they are ready for pick up at the launch station. This allows for even greater convenience and speed of purchase.

Online Ordering

The web site companion to the launch stations enables customers to order their meals in ten seconds. They can then pick it up on their way home from work. This interactive component reinforces the innovative nature of the product and connects with the target audience in a very functional   75B
way. Laughton elaborates, "Ordering over the web makes things simpler. We're just trying to find new ways to cut time down. When you go there, along with the menu are little treats, interesting nuggets, a listing of events, for example. Something which encourages you to have a good time. Technology makes life easier. It makes you believe that things are possible."

WOLFF OLINS

Robbie Laughton describes the interdisciplinary nature of WO, "Think of Wolff Olins as three circles overlapping. The three circles represent strategy with consultants; creativity with designers or collective thinkers; and management with account directors. With the mixture of these three you achieve a little bit of drama school, art school and economics school, with some psychology thrown in. We all get out there together. Sometimes the designer comes up with the strategy and the account directors come up with some creative applications."

The Wolff Olins web site has informative content about branding and the firm. Images that fade into one another add movement and interest.

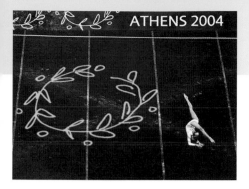

Athens 2004 Olympic Committee: Embracing the World

This inspirational brand succinctly communicates the purity and simplicity of the original Greek Games. With Athens, the Games are coming home to Greece, and the brand expresses a vision that is inclusive and worldwide.

World Gold Council: The Sun on Earth

By the end of the 1990s consumers had begun to see gold jewelry as ostentatious, old-fashioned, even tacky. In early 2000, World Gold Council approached Wolff Olins to help put gold back where it belongs. Within twelve months they launched an emotionally persuasive brand repositioning by placing gold at the heart of people's lives.

Tate Museums: Look Again, Think Again

With Tate, Wolff Olins provided a distinctive, worldwide brand that broadened the museum's appeal and conveyed its forward-thinking approach to experiencing art.

"We work for clients who believe in themselves to put something good into the world, to try to change their sectors and lead the way— not just make money."
—Robbie Laughton

The Approach: Turn your office into a creative think tank.

CarboneSmolanAgency
Sesame

Location:
New York, NY

Principals:
Ken Carbone
Leslie Smolan

Staff:
25 professionals

CARBONE

SMOLAN

The Firm

In 1977, Ken Carbone and Leslie Smolan opened a small design firm in downtown New York. They decided from the very beginning that they did not want to focus on a specific area of design but remain diverse in their capabilities. Ken Carbone elaborates, "We liked the full palette of possibilities and challenges that could be presented to a designer in two dimensions, three dimensions and now in the digital realm. That has given us an opportunity to both build professional and personal careers enriched by a multitude of different kinds of experiences."

Initially focusing on cultural institutions, today Carbone Smolan Agency (CSA) works for an elite and international group of clients. Over the years they have developed a reputation for being able to successfully design signage programs that guide visitors through complicated museums and other institutions. Carbone continues, "Today, our work is generally divided into five sectors: financial services, professional services, kids products and services, luxury marketers and cultural institutions."

Philosophically, CSA is truly a creative think tank. "We pride ourselves on being thinking designers. Yes, we are interested in what it's going to look like in the end, but we're equally interested in the strategy that gets us there. So it's been a long time since someone gave us the typed brief that says, 'We want a 24-page brochure and here's a stack of photographs; put it together.'"

68B

Workshop

sesame
workshop™

The new logo, above, communicates "a creative place where people can come together to invent and experiment in pursuit of a common goal."

The Client Project

Some 30 years ago, Children's Television Workshop (CTW) changed the face of children's television. Unfortunately, CTW had little recognition as the brain power behind the innovative show *Sesame Street*. "I asked, 'Who's the company that brought you Cookie Monster, Big Bird and Elmo?' Everyone said Sesame Street, when it was Children's Television Workshop," explains Carbone.

There was another reason CTW was interested in rebranding. They were evolving from a television-based entity to an all media-based organization. The word "television" within the name had become a liability. "The companies they partner with, who are also sometimes considered their competitors—Disney, Nickelodeon, Learning Channel, Discovery—are not so linked to television."

CSA came to the project toward the end of the renaming exercise. CTW had come up with three possibilities: Sesame Co., Sesame Workshop and Sesame Unlimited. They were leaning toward the latter. "We asked them to reconsider Sesame Workshop because it borrowed from their premiere property, but also it borrowed from the previous name." The board of directors approved.

Historically, CTW had used word marks, either spelling out their name or using the initials. They communicated to CSA that they felt a symbol wasn't necessary. After initial testing, CSA felt differently: "The word mark alone was not strong visually. Also, it was clear that the market was essentially preschool, and we should develop a brand that was an icon—that children could embrace."

Tarzana Narrow
ABCDEFGHIJKLMNOPQRSTUVWXYZ
abcdefghijklmnopqrstuvwxyz
1234567890

Tarzana Narrow Bold
ABCDEFGHIJKLMNOPQRSTUVWXYZ
abcdefghijklmnopqrstuvwxyz
1234567890

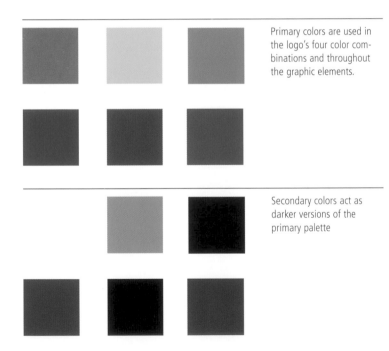

Primary colors are used in the logo's four color combinations and throughout the graphic elements.

Secondary colors act as darker versions of the primary palette

The Brand Rules and Tools

As stated in the brand manual, Sesame Workshop's mission "is to create innovative, engaging content that maximizes the educational power of all media to help children reach their highest potential." The organization represents innovation, optimism, knowledge and diversity, and the brand manual clearly outlines visual standards that communicate and uphold these goals. It also clearly describes the brand personality: "The workshop identity is laced with a fundamental educational mission complementary to the brand turf of the premiere property, *Sesame Street*—not too cute or saccharin but definitely kid friendly. The lights are turned on at Sesame Workshop—the brand is luminescent, bright and inviting. It says 'Join us.' The editorial voice is clever and witty and is a lean backdrop to the variety inherent in the properties."

Sesame Workshop
Project Team:
Ken Carbone, Creative Director
Justin Peters, Design Director
Christa Bianchi, Senior Designer
Tom Sopkovich, Designer
Cliff Doerzbacher, Photographer

Tarzana Narrow was the primary font chosen to reflect the brand. A serif face, Slimbach, is used as a secondary typeface. As the brand manual describes, these two fonts were chosen because "they have a modest, approachable presence while feeling modern, innovative and slightly quirky."

Along with color and typography, CSA developed a palette of shapes and a "spark" pattern that is derived from the logo itself. These elements are a wonderfully expressive part of the identity system, and they add life and variety to the applications.

"Shapes are simple, friendly, recognizable.
Colors are bold; scale change is dramatic."
–Sesame Workshop Standards Manual

Process sketches showing word mark investigations, top; and icon refinement, bottom.

The Process

CSA's general process has four phases: foundation, creative strategy, brand implementation and documentation. Over the last decade their philosophy toward problem solving has changed. Carbone says, "Design is often seen as a problem-solving exercise, and I want to get out of the problem-solving business. I want to be in the opportunity-creating business. We're not here to simply solve the client's problems; we're here to identify new opportunities. Sometimes they should just forget the problems they have, make a right turn and go in a totally different direction."

For CSA, testing is also important. They conducted a competitive analysis for Sesame Workshop, comparing their logo concepts with other prominent children's entertainment companies. This proved their point about the use of a word mark vs. an icon, and it helped in the refinement phase.

Carbone continues, "We did a number of different iterations of the house. We started to diminish the importance of the name. We chose a typeface—Tarzana—which has a playfulness about it, but we didn't want anything that looked like a kid drew it. We wanted it to have a bit of sophistication. We tested various ideas with parents and some other partner groups. We asked, 'How do you feel about this house? What does it say to you?'"

As the mark developed they did more extensive application studies, such as CDs, book covers and packaging. "In order to survive in some pretty visually competitive environments, we simplified the mark. We reduced the number of elements in the house and simplified the color scheme. The result was a visually stronger and easy-to-use icon."

20B-23B

69B

54A

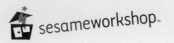

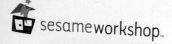

The Perfect Brand Launch

Sesame Workshop launched the brand over a weekend. Everything was cleaned out the Friday before and all the new materials were put into place by that Monday morning. This made for a clean and cost-effective transition.

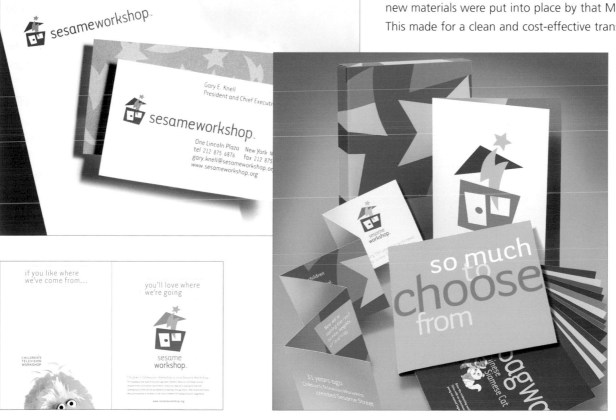

Print applications for Sesame Workshop.

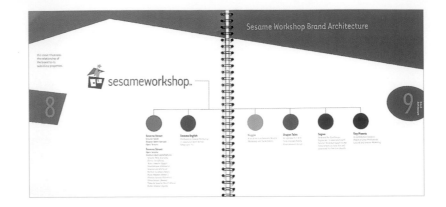

Through its playful use of shape, color and typography, the standards manual was intended to model the look and feel of the brand.

The conference booth for Sesame Workshop was one of the first expressions of the two-dimensional mark in three-dimensional terms. The booth has a jaunty, angular cut-out shape and none of the walls are at ninety degrees, adding to the playfulness. The angularity made a wonderful visual connection to the mark design and also made the booth stand out from other booths.

Carbone describes the launch: "It was a wonderful thing to watch. This was a significant move—for an underfunded organization to make the change overnight. It's the way to do it. They had everything set up, their press conference and press materials were ready to go. When you clicked on the web site that following week the new site loaded. The press kit had all of the information about the name change and the heritage of the organization. We had a nice box that contained a T-shirt with a black-and-white outline version of the mark and a set of fabric markers for kids to color in the logo. It all generated a lot of excitement about the change."

There was also a very important document to build internal support for the change—a thank you brochure from the CEO to the employees which acknowledged their hard work in building a great company, and gave encouragement in continuing to build an even stronger brand with the new name. It also explained the reasoning behind the name change and restated the mission. This was a truly important element. Evolving brands when you have many people in the organization with deep roots is touchy. Carbone says, "You have to make sure you are communicating and thanking those people in order to gain their support to move forward."

71B

Primary, above, and secondary pages, right, for the Sesame Workshop web site.

The Influence of Technology

Technology played an important role in some of the design decisions for the Sesame Workshop project. For instance, the color palette was developed for print, web and TV. CSA had to define the translation of those colors across media, making sure they remained constant and vivid. Animation was also an important consideration. Carbone describes, "If you look at the animation at the end of the show close, the house in the logo animates with the roof flying upward in a sprinkle of stars. The fireworks fall down between the letters, and the letters fill in with the color. So the two-dimensional work that we did translated very well to the other media."

46B-53B

Screen resolution was another important consideration. "A lot of the smaller pieces of the earlier mark probably would have been lost at low resolution. We tested it along the way to make sure it was going to hold up," says Carbone.

identity

The playful energy of the identity materials for Carbone Smolan Agency is complemented by clarity and thoughtfulness. Color and typography work together to communicate a confident and approachable feel.

csa

Carbone Smolan Agency

Playful promotional pieces like the yo-yo, fris-bee, and shopping bag communicate that "we work hard, but we know how to have fun, too."

Animation and audio play key roles in the design of the CSA web site. As an introduction to each section of the site, color-coded bands emanate from the rotating logo. Rhythmic music complements the rippling motion.

"I make it my business to get to know the prospective client.
There may not be an assignment right away,
but if I have an ongoing dialogue with them,
I can start to understand the full extent of their needs
and how to respond to them.
Then, when a project comes along, I'm primed
to offer more strategic ideas."
– Ken Carbone

CHILDREN

The Approach: Think broadly and deeply, making an emotional connection.

Morris Creative

Hasbro

Location:

San Diego, CA

Principal:

Steven Morris

Staff:

6 professionals

The Firm

"In our office lobby there is a bright, shiny steel trash can filled with design awards. It acts as a symbol to our clients and to us, of what is important in our work. Peer recognition—although important—does not rank as the highest element on our importance totem pole. These competitions do not ask, 'Did the creative work for your client?' or 'Was the creative effective?'"

For Morris Creative, the true gauge of their work is its effectiveness for the client and audience. Their philosophy and process are represented by their motto: "Think. Feel. Work.™" They think broadly and deeply about the overall brand presence, not just the aesthetics. They feel that developing an emotional connection between the sender and receiver of the information creates memorable solutions, and that intuition is an important element in the creative process. And they work to create a tangible product that is consistent in design and message.

Steve Morris started the firm in 1994 after moving from Washington, D.C. to San Diego. "I started in one bedroom of the house, then moved to a second bedroom, and then into the living room as well. When I started having client meetings with my dogs barking, I figured it was time to get a studio space." Morris Creative has remained small in size but not in capabilities. They offer full-service solutions to a broad range of clients.

onka

Tonka

Primary mark.

The Client Project

The brand manual describes the start of Tonka: "In 1946, in the basement of a small schoolhouse in Mound, Minnesota, Lynn E. Baker, Avery Crounse and Alvin Tesch founded Mound Metalcraft Co….The primary production was a major output of hoes, rakes and shovels, along with tie, hat and shoe racks. Toy production was a sideline. During their first year…Mound produced their first two toys, a steam shovel and crane." Their success with these products grew into Tonka Toys, named after Lake Minnetonka.

The founding premise of Tonka trucks was to provide consumers with a toy that was durable, reasonably priced and, of course, FUN! In 1991, the Tonka brand became a part of Hasbro, Inc., and Tonka continues to be number one in the category of nonpowered trucks.

Before coming to Morris for a brand overhaul, Tonka was perceived as the "little yellow truck" company. Morris' job was to breathe a new progressive life into the Tonka brand so it could effectively compete with the more interactive toys in the marketplace. 71B With a well-defined core market of three- to six-year-old boys, and an extremely high international brand recognition, the old brand perception had a lot going for it. However, it needed updating so people would realize that the brand was diversified and had a wide variety of both traditional and interactive toys.

Secondary marks with a border added.

Futura Condensed Extra Bold
ABCDEFGHIJKLMNOPQRSTUVWXYZ
abcdefghijklmnopqrstuvwxyz
1234567890

Futura Extra Bold
ABCDEFGHIJKLMNOPQRSTUVWXYZ
abcdefghijklmnopqrstuvwxyz
1234567890

MACHINE
ABCDEFGHIJKLMNOPQRSTUVWXYZ
ABCDEFGHIJKLMNOPQRSTUVWXYZ
1234567890

Toxic Waste
ABCDEFGHIJKLMNOPQRSTUVWXYZ
abcdefghijklmnopqrstuvwxyz
1234567890

Compacta Bold Italic
ABCDEFGHIJKLMNOPQRSTUVWXYZ
abcdefghijklmnopqrstuvwxyz
1234567890

The Brand Rules and Tools

The typographic family for the Tonka brand has a lot of variety to add flexibility and to capture the playful quality of the products. All the icons, images, patterns and borders can be downloaded from an interactive style guide, but the fonts are another story. You can't license another company's fonts, so Morris had to pick ones that were readily available through popular font houses. As Morris explains, "We tried to pick fonts that were relatively universal, at least for the core group of fonts. The secondary fonts support the line and have a lot more flavor." Futura, in a variety of weights, is the main font for the brand. Machine, Toxic Waste, and Compacta complement the classic geometry of Futura and add a lot of variety to the system.

The color palette is also broad, offering a good sampling of primaries, as you would expect, with secondaries and neutrals. Metallic colors are also used, when possible, to add interest.

Hasbro Tonka Project Team:

Steve Morris, Creative Director, Designer,
   Illustrator

Tom Davie, Designer, Illustrator

Tracy Meiners, Designer

Shelly Hays, Designer

Sean Riley, Programmer

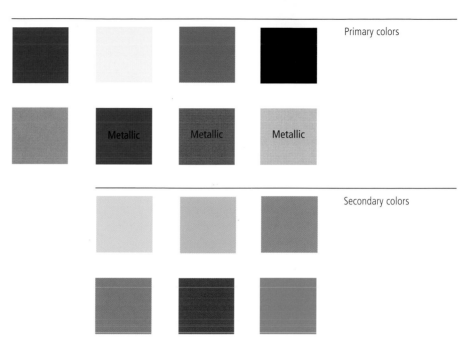

Primary colors

Metallic   Metallic   Metallic

Secondary colors

The Morris Creative team designed a wide range of icons, patterns, borders and imagery for implementation. As Morris explains, "The elements of the brand identity are applied to everything from a sleeping bag to a backpack to school materials, to interactive games and clothing. A lot of considerations were taken into account regarding how the end user would need to use the elements. We wanted to enable them and empower them with as much flexibility as possible while creating clear boundaries in which to design."

A sampling of the diverse set of icons developed by Morris Creative for the Tonka promotions and products.

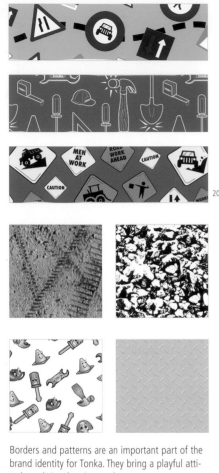

Borders and patterns are an important part of the brand identity for Tonka. They bring a playful attitude and visual variety to the system.

Morris Creative also created a series of line art and full-color illustrations for use on Tonka packaging and promotions.

20B-23B

The Process

Morris Creative was hired directly by Hasbro's Corporate Creative. They also reported to Hasbro Licensing, Hasbro's Boys Brand Group and the U.K. Group in London. Having four "masters" was a creative challenge because they all had different perspectives on the definition of the brand, how it related to the parent company and how the rebirth of the brand should take place. Another interesting challenge was that, as Morris describes, "Hasbro hired us without meeting us. We were forced on both ends to hit the ground running. We had to try to get to know one another as well as figure out our working styles and define the objectives. So we started off with a series of creative briefs that we developed through interviews."

"The process begins by engaging in traditional audience research, understanding the client, understanding their brand and then taking that and spilling it over into understanding the emotional qualities of the brand—the emotional intellect. Then the work, the application of the brand, makes it all tangible."

The Tonka Brand Manual is available in an interactive CD format, which allows download of logos, patterns, borders and illustrations. Morris also created a printed manual that includes the same information.

Print vs. Interactive Applications

Morris Creative designed two versions of the style guide, one in print and the other interactive. Morris explains, "The purpose of two guides is really from a useability standpoint. Because it is a style guide, it goes out to anyone who licenses the Tonka product brand. The print version acts as an encyclopedia of all the elements that make up the brand and includes the brand history. The reason for the interactive version is to allow users to extract artwork." The interactive version is a complete duplication of the print version, plus most of it is downloadable.

He continues, "Once you understand what the brand is through the printed version, you can go to the interactive version and quickly scroll through the different iconography, patterns and borders and extract them for use. So the interactive version really exists in support of the printed version."

18B

46B-53B

65A

The Tonka interactive style guide uses audio of working machines and animation of elements on the screen to bring the Tonka brand to life.

The interactive version also acts as an example of how new interactive pieces for Tonka should be executed. Hasbro Interactive, for instance, refers to the design of the CD presentation for styling new interactive games.

After a lot of thought, Morris decided to change the page orientation from the print version. The screen, of course, is horizontal, but the book itself is vertical. "We thought a lot about the size and the fact that we wanted a flip-up version for the book. We wanted something that was personal and could sit on someone's desk for a long time without taking up too much space." The cover material gives a unique and playful touch to the presentation and is very functional. It's made of a thick but flexible rubber, and has the texture of tire treads. This heavy cover also provides a protective backing for the CD that is attached to the back cover.

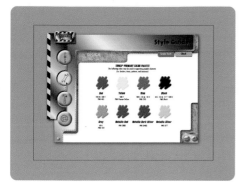

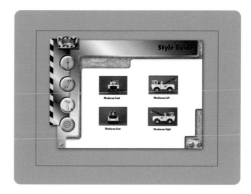

D E S I G N   T I P
Creative briefs can be a very important communication tool between a client and a design firm. Before Steve Morris internally assigns a job he has his client approve the brief, which clearly defines the project and objectives. "It helps to continually communicate and articulate where we are and our objectives throughout the process."

The Influence of Technology

This project presented several technical challenges. With downloaded artwork, for instance, the Morris Creative team had to be very concerned about the file type. They wanted the downloadable artwork to be scalable (a vector-based file) rather than a TIFF file. The illustrations, for example, were originally done by hand, so they had to scan them in and recreate them in Illustrator. An easier process would have been to just scan them in 18B and give the user a TIFF, but that's not as flexible in terms of useability.

In discussing the balance between print and interactive media Morris concludes, "The 46B-53B computer screen is always going to be a different experience from the printed page or packaging. I think print will always play a role in communication, especially if you want to get very personal with your communication. Interactive work will continue to grow, but I don't think it will ever replace print."

67A

identity

Morris Creative has a wide range of identity and promotional materials. They focus on fun giveaway items that drive their philosophy home.

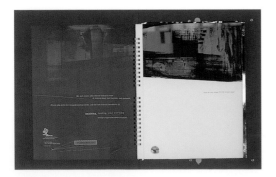

Developing meaningful human relationships is at the core of Steven Morris' personal and professional philosophy. "We are trying to have close relationships with our consumer audiences—relationships that are highly ethical, highly communicative, involve a lot of emotion, and are a whole lot of fun. This enriches our lives and our ability to communicate effectively."

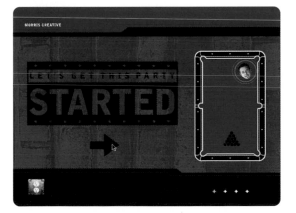

The "serious" (top) vs. the "fun" (bottom) sections of the Morris Creative web site communicate their philosophy, "Take your work seriously, but never take yourself seriously." There is a clear distinction between the two sections, balanced by links in typography, texture and use of black.

Think. Feel. Work.™

The Approach: Balance your rational and intuitive sides for dual appeal.

Iconologic

Kilpatrick

Location:

Atlanta, GA

Principals:

Brad Copeland

Ward Copeland

Ben Friedman

Staff:

22 professionals

The Firm

"It began with an idea. It grew and evolved for over twenty years. The name became Iconologic...it was inspired by a seventeenth-century Renaissance book entitled *Iconologia*. Written by Caesar Ripa, the book served as a guide for translating symbolism in Renaissance art." President and CEO Brad Copeland has formed several design firms, including Cooper Copeland, Copeland Design, Copeland Hirther and Brain Sandwich, Copeland Hirther's digital interactive arm. To enhance collaboration and integration, the latter two firms joined in 2000, becoming Iconologic. Creative Director Mike Weikert

32B-37B 🌐 explains, "We call ourselves a brand collaborative. We have the ability to integrate disciplines across media."

A firm distinction is their marriage of design and writing. Associate Creative Director and writer Juliet D'Ambrosio elaborates, "Writing and design are absolutely co-dependent upon each other. We have always had writers, not only on staff, but in leadership positions. We don't start an identity process without having a writer involved."

"Iconologic's process is a meeting place where the rational and the intuitive become one. You need to speak to both the rational side of the consumer's mind and to their emotional side. You have to have dual appeal. We do that by distilling the brand down to its essence and creating a message that is both visually and verbally compelling. It speaks with a big, single idea," explains Weikert.

Stockton

KILPATRICK STOCKTON LLP

The Client Project

Kilpatrick Stockton is a 125-year-old law firm that competes on both a national and global level with a strong presence throughout the Southeast and offices in Europe. The full-service law firm emphasizes intellectual property and prides themselves on having innovative clients like Harley-Davidson, who they actually assisted in protecting the trademarked sound of the revving engine. They were also responsible for trademarking the curvy shape of the original Coca-Cola bottle.

Iconologic's task was to rescue Kilpatrick Stockton from an out-of-date perception that they were a big, conservative, regional, stodgy law firm and change it to an updated perception of what they had actually become—a global firm that practices cutting-edge law and possesses a progressive and open culture. Iconologic's creative challenge was "to figure out a way to combine both the innovative, forward-thinking side with their strong, historical foundation."

"All media are activated to create momentum around the Kilpatrick Stockton message; the program brings the brand's 'Traditions of Innovation' message to life through advertising, interactive, environmental, print collateral, motion media and 'The Innovation Continuum'—a continuous, interactive timeline that adds dimension to the strategic positioning through client stories and firm facts," explains Iconologic's web site.

KILPATRICK STOCKTON LLP
Attorneys at Law

KILPATRICK STOCKTON LLP
TRADITIONS OF INNOVATION

 KILPATRICK STOCKTON LLP
In Business With the World

18B

46B-53B

The primary mark (top), the secondary marks with tags (middle two logos), and the previous mark (directly above).

Berthold Akzidenz Grotesk Medium
ABCDEFGHIJKLMNOPQRSTUVWXYZ
abcdefghijklmnopqrstuvwxyz
1234567890

Minion Regular
ABCDEFGHIJKLMNOPQRSTUVWXYZ
abcdefghijklmnopqrstuvwxyz
1234567890

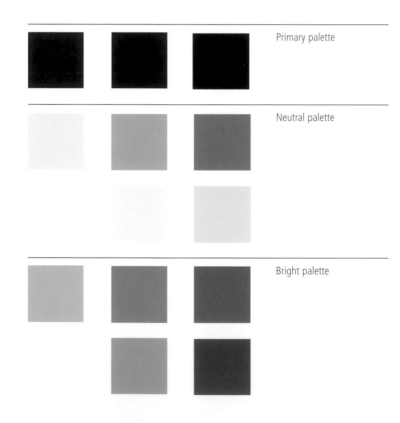

Primary palette

Neutral palette

Bright palette

The Brand Rules and Tools

The brand manual states that "the Kilpatrick Stockton brand creates a unique, powerful position that distinguishes the firm within a highly competitive marketplace. The brand builds on the firm's primary strengths, communicating a nuanced balance of heritage, sophistication and innovation. Some key brand messages of Kilpatrick Stockton are: smart, trusted, traditional, multidisciplined, visionary, global, entrepreneurial, creative, confident, progressive."

Designer Lea Friedman elaborates on the specific design decisions. "The serif typeface Minion was chosen because of its traditional serif form and large versatile family of weights and styles, while Akzidenz Grotesk was chosen as its more modern complement. Akzidenz Grotesk is used for impact in headlines and as an unexpected alternative to the traditional law firm aesthetic. Together, these faces support both sides of the spectrum of the firm's 'Traditions of Innovation' tagline."

Kilpatrick Stockton Project Team:
Brad Copeland, President & CEO
Ben Friedman, Partner
David Woodward, Partner
Mike Weikert, Creative Director
Juliet D'Ambrosio, Writer
Lea Friedman, Designer
Drew Brown, Account Executive
Ken Schles, Photographer

The color palette is bold yet sophisticated, breaking the mold of the traditional muted law firm aesthetic. The primary palette is based on the core identity colors, bright reds and black, while the bright palette serves as a vibrant accent for the brand—and is used for Kilpatrick Stockton's recruiting materials' younger, law school-based audience. The neutral palette is used for both recruiting and firm applications, bringing sophistication and balance to the brighter colors.

The photographic style captures the law firm's energy through a photojournalistic "day-in-the-life" approach.

smart, trusted, traditional, multidisciplined, visionary, global, entrepreneurial, creative, confident, progressive

Kilpatrick|Stockton LLP

The Process

The Kilpatrick Stockton project closely followed the classic Iconologic process: "Define, Design and Build." During the "Define" stage they dive into the project and learn everything they can about the brand, the client and the problem. In the "Design" stage they create the look and voice of the brand. "Build" moves into the brand evolution, which looks ahead to what's next—where the brand will go in the next two to five years, and what steps are needed to take it there. "We see the process as a cycle with no real end. It must continue to evolve and grow, so we constantly foster these partnerships with our clients. We are always thinking two steps ahead of what is currently on the table," explains Weikert.

    One unique feature of this project was the sequence of applications. The logo came first, of course, but the supplemental recruiting web site came before the main web site. Its bolder, edgier look pushed the broad-based firm materials in a more innovative direction.

20B-23B

71B

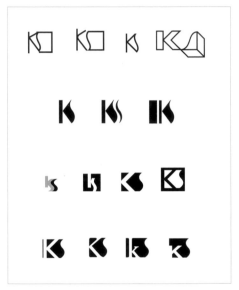

Logo sketches, left and above, show the evolution of the team's ideas.

The stationery package, top, report cover, above, and advertisement, right, are a representative sample of the print materials for the overall firm identity. They reflect the balance between the traditional and the progressive.

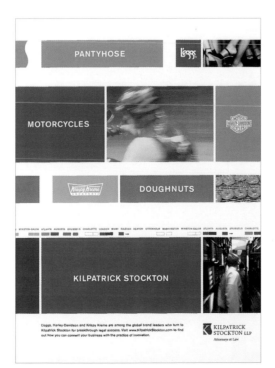

The Value of Branding

"As the legal profession becomes ever more media-savvy and competition for clients—and excellent attorneys—increasingly intense, a strong brand presence has become essential for law firms to compete on a global scale," explains the text on Iconologic's web site.

Only recently have law firms started to market themselves. Not long ago, it did not follow their professional etiquette standards. Such professionals have recently discovered the value and power of branding to attract potential clients and potential employees.

Branding also became invaluable for Kilpatrick Stockton in communicating the global nature of the firm. Although based in Atlanta, it was very important for Kilpatrick Stockton to communicate its global impact. Both the design and the text had to represent the firm as an international player, using a balanced creative approach.

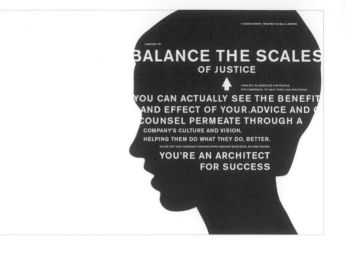

Kilpatrick Stockton's recruiting brochure, above and right, speaks to a younger, more progressive student audience and integrates design and writing in an innovative fashion.

Developing a recruiting package that was edgier and bolder, alongside the materials to represent the company as a whole, was a unique challenge. As D'Ambrosio explains, "I was continually surprised by the way the client pushed us to a really edgy look. Because of our preconceived notions, I think our initial design would have been more conservative." This particular client is a good example of Iconologic's philosophy to engage the client from the beginning of the project so they are part of the process.

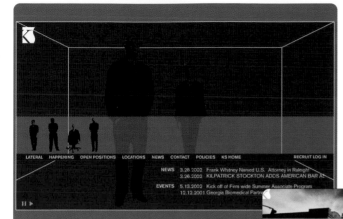

46B-53B

DESIGN TIP

"Just because we can make logos spin doesn't necessarily mean that we should make logos spin. If it's going to spin it should be spinning because it helps to communicate the brand message or it helps to solve the problem." – Mike Weikert

In the recruiting web site, above and right, the bold, high contrast images of men and women connect with the viewer on a personal level while maintaining an edgy, abstract quality.

The Influence of the Web

David Woodward talks about Iconologic's approach to interactive projects: "We go through a detailed design phase that results in an information architecture. In this phase we ask a lot of questions about users and the client. The content and function really influence the design. This is all written up in a document, a kind of blueprint."

The firm's timeline is used both in print and interactive designs to reinforce the balance between the progressive and the traditional. The web allows for a more dimensional feel, and the interactive component gives a true feeling of time. In the print application, the project team used an accordion fold to simulate the effect, giving the sense of continuity to the static form. Friedman states another example of the web's influence: "The recruiting web site had a lot of interesting color transparency overlays. For print, we overprinted Pantone colors on imagery to achieve the same look."

75B

In the firm web site, as with all of the materials, writing and design are seamlessly integrated. The writing voice and personality complements and supports the design solution. The interactive timeline is integrated into the image bar in the top half of the page.

identity

Iconologic's business cards use an innovative shape, embossing and metallic ink to communicate the progressive and forward-thinking nature of the firm.

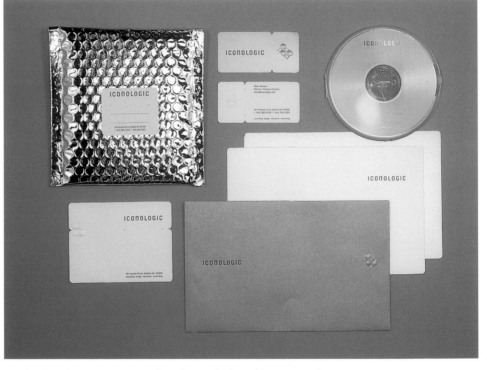

Iconologic's applications contrast metallic with matte finishes, adding variety and interest.

"I think the first step is developing a partnership with your client. You have to learn about their brand and about the essence. We try to develop that brand's vocabulary and consistently look ahead for ways to achieve those goals beyond what the client might be thinking. We try to refer to our clients as our partners because the goal is to engage them in the process so they feel passionate about the brand ownership and executions."
–Mike Weikert

+ ICONOLOGIC +

The web site uses animation and compelling imagery to bring Iconologic's ideas to life. The site content includes the firm history, information about partners, a client list, a description of their process and services, a portfolio of work, a media kit and contact information. An especially informative portion of the site focuses on five case studies. These detailed examples communicate Iconologic's depth of approach and solutions.

Iconologic's color palette is limited and effective. White and metallic silver are used throughout the materials with bright blue acting as an accent.

"Iconologic is a brand collaborative—
we define, design and build brands."
–www.iconologic.com

MONIGLE ASSOCIATES

Monigle Assoc

TierOne Bank

The Approach: Work with the client to get early input.

Location:
Denver, CO

Principals:
Rick Jacobs
Glenn Monigle
Kurt Monigle
Tom Webb

Staff:
65 professionals

WEBB — JACOBS — SURINE

The Firm

Founded in 1972, Denver-based Monigle Associates ranks among the largest branding firms in the country. Over the past thirty years, Monigle has implemented branding solutions for national and international clients. The company delivers brand strategy and positioning, naming conventions, identity and logo design, online brand management tools, and environmental design, signage and implementation services.

Monigle's philosophy focuses on strategy. As their capabilities brochure describes, "While the needs and objectives of each of our clients are unique, the goal of each project is the same—to ensure that all brand elements and core communications are aligned and working in concert to communicate a focused, distinct and relevant set of messages to all key audiences." Unique services include the development of extensive online management systems and brand training workshops for management and employees.

Principal Tom Webb describes Monigle's approach: "We form teams for each assignment, which include specialists appropriate to the particular business or industry. Commonly, this design team is made up of web, graphic and industrial designers, each member contributing ideas to the overall project." Designer Scott Surine adds, "Pulling two-dimensional and three-dimensional designers together allows us to think seamlessly and have a clear understanding of multiple disciplines."

73B

54B

TierOne^{SM} BANK

The Client Project

The Monigle web site tells the story of First Federal Lincoln Bank: "First Federal Lincoln Bank was in a quandary. Their success had outgrown their name. 'Lincoln' (Lincoln, Nebraska) would not support a business with fifty-eight offices in three states and 'Federal' conjured up 1980s savings and loan association images. The challenge was how to create a brand that was distinctive while capturing the organization's brand essence. Name development and visual identity design culminated in the TierOne Bank brand. The very essence of the name suggests 'top tier,' 'industry leader,' leading edge' and 'top-level service.'"

Project Manager Gary Naifeh says, "The goal was to work diligently through a variety of names. TierOne was descriptive and distinctive. It was a perfect fit for an organization that prides itself on an extra level of service and continuing growth in product offerings." The new word mark incorporated typography and colors that exude dignity, progressive attitude, elegance and timelessness.

Monigle applied this new brand to an online standards manual, facility signage, ATMs, credit/debit cards, digital media applications and print collateral to project a consistent brand message. Their Brand Ambassador^{SM} Workshops were used to communicate the brand message to all TierOne employees. This enabled everyone to convey the brand's message effectively and efficiently through their conversations and actions.

Primary mark in color, top, and black and white, above.

Previous logo.

Centennial
ABCDEFGHIJKLMNOPQRSTUVWXYZ
abcdefghijklmnopqrstuvwxyz
1234567890

Meta
ABCDEFGHIJKLMNOPQRSTUVWXYZ
abcdefghijklmnopqrstuvwxyz
1234567890

Primary palette

Monigle developed this support graphic coined the "TierLine" to extend the system and further communicate the brand attributes of "top-level service" and "industry leader." Variations are shown from the top: linear, pattern, shape, color and collage.

The Brand Rules and Tools

The bold colors and precise angles of the TierOne identity effectively convey the forward momentum of the company. The visuals also imply the bank's commitment to state-of-the-art technology. Complemented by the new tagline, "Taking the extra step," TierOne's brand comprehensively and cohesively communicates their message.

Monigle's design development stressed the need for system flexibility. Two type families—one serif, Centennial, and one sans serif, Meta—were chosen to bring variety while maintaining a level of consistency in the identity package.

The inherent flexibility of the system is also evident in the accompanying graphic elements. The various expressions of the "TierLine," left, can be applied to any number of applications to add unity and variety. The standards proclaim, "With adherence to only a few guidelines, the limitations of how the TierLine can be expressed are only restricted by the designer's imagination."

In addition to the TierLine, visually compelling collages were developed by Monigle designer Marcus Fitzgibbons. These images, right, were "created to be interchangeably used on a variety of applications and designed to set a metaphorical stage for the TierOne story."

achieve
advantage
commitment
excel
leader
perform
premiere

20B-23B

Process sketches above include five different directions, left to right: simple word mark, pinnacle sub-symbol, monogram symbol, regional imagery, and upward progression. "We didn't want the graphics to get in the way of the simplicity and the strength of the name. Secondly, with a manufactured word like TierOne, legibility becomes more important," explains Surine.

The Process

Once the name TierOne had been selected, Monigle went about an extensive process of idea generation. Surine describes, "It was well defined that we needed a word mark to establish the new name. Our initial design effort included 200 to 250 ideas. The ideas were narrowed to several distinct directions (shown above)."

Monigle shared many initial concepts with the client, not for approval, but purely for discussing the merits of each direction. They invited their clients' input early in the process because they felt the client was truly a partner—they were all in this together. There were also a small number of decision makers, so "design by committee" was not an issue. "TierOne appreciated the process because it allowed them to have early contribution and buy-in. It paid off huge dividends in the end," concludes Webb.

TierOne℠

BANK

Employee Name
Primary Title

TierOne Bank
1234 Street Address, Suite 100
City Name, ST 12345-6789
555.123.4567 Phone
800.123.8765 Toll Free
555.123.7654 Fax
ename@tieronebank.com

Business cards, above, and credit cards, right, are two of the most prominent applications in the system. Clean, clear typography complements the logo and bold colors.

Check Card

TierOne℠

BANK

0102 0304 0506 0708
0102
2000 VALID THRU 10/03
CARDMEMBER SINCE
CARDHOLDER NAME

VISA

The Implementation

With the perception that they were an old-line bank, always doing a good job but just under the radar, TierOne needed a radical change in their market presence. "They have awakened to the population. The public doesn't see TierOne as a sleepy little company anymore. It has given them a chance to tell the public about their vision for the future and plans for expansion and growth of services," says Webb. He continues, "We take a holistic approach to design in creating a unique design system for our clients. The use of typography, shape, spatial relationships, graphic elements including patterns, textures, customized imagery, color and texture all support the idea of TierOne being new and in the top level of service."

54B

"When something is elevated to brand status, there is an emotional glue between the company and its constituency."
–Rick Jacobs

The sign family for TierOne ranged from an enormous sign on their headquarters, which took two cranes to lift into place, to little signs on branch banks in small-town Nebraska. Monigle had to be very sensitive to context. A big red sign may or may not be appropriate given the size and culture of a town. They created a number of approaches to maintain the integrity of the brand while accommodating the needs of different locations.

ROBERT W. ANDREWS
123 YOUR STREET
ANYWHERE, U.S.A. 12345

101

00-00/000

Date

Pay to the
Order of

$

Dollars

Security features
are included.
Details on back.

TierOne℠
BANK

Client Name
1234 Street Address, Suite 100
City Name, ST 12345-6789

For

MP

⑈000000000⑈ 123⑉4567⑊ 0101

Clarke American

TierOne Bank checks.

The Brand Ambassador℠ Workshops

"From a thousand voices to a voice of thousands"—Monigle's Brand Ambassador℠ Workshops are individually tailored to meet a company's unique needs. They are meant to help clients understand how to fully implement their total brand. For TierOne they did a series of workshops. Gary Naifeh explains, "We held a three hour session with thirty-plus vice presidents discussing the key issues evolving around the brand and how they needed to assume the leadership as the key brand ambassadors for the organization. We also held a series of programs for supervisory and management personnel, and they in turn did a series of employee workshops at each of the branches. It took approximately three weeks to take everyone through the process, and it was very effective. At the end of the three weeks everyone was in alignment, knew what the brand stood for, knew what their obligations were and how their behaviors needed to reflect the brand."

They also did a very interesting assignment with the executives. They had each of the executives do a work plan describing, for themselves and for their teams, what they wanted to accomplish over a period of thirty, sixty and ninety days in order to have everyone live the brand. These goals were noted along with their benefits to the organization.

The TierOne Bank identityManager™ includes a wealth of visual and verbal content for employees, vendors and partners. The home page, above, allows log-in to authorized users of the site. Other pages teach employees about identity standards and provide application templates and examples.

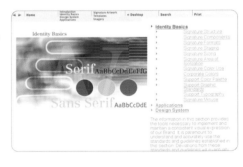

The identityManager™

To aid in the implementation of the brand, Monigle created the first full-feature online brand management tool kit called the identityManager™. As Rick Jacobs describes, "We used to create those three-ring binders that would gather dust. We are now using web technology to house all a company's branded assets—the tools, templates, digital imagery and brand decision tools. These elements are accessible to all of the employees and their vendors and partners all over the world, and it is password coded to ensure security."

This management system drives home the importance of the brand assets and makes it easy for management and employees to implement the brand immediately. Updates and changes to company standards can be distributed efficiently and consistently using this online tool. As employees become familiar and comfortable with the wide range of information and assets, the tool also ensures continuity in implementation over the long term.

75B

87A

identity

Boldly colored folders and brochures contrast with the clean stationery set.

Monigle's own identity materials speak to their philosophy of strategic design. They term their approach *brandscaping*, which focuses on identifying a company's brand essence. "Brand essence is what you stand for, what sets you apart and makes you unique," says Tom Webb. The core identity tools—name, design, brand structure—emanate from the brand essence. Beyond this are the communications elements and specific applications. All elements combine together to create the brandscape.

Monigle has several different types of promotional vehicles, including case study sheets and postcards, brochures and "Identity Update" newsletters. The "modular" nature of these pieces means Monigle can easily tailor presentations to connect with client needs.

Monigle's web site uses color, typography, motion and sound to communicate their brand essence. The site consistently delivers their message through detailed content and clearly organized pages. The BrandWire portion of the site breaks slightly from the format to identify it as the separate "newsletter" portion of the site.

Landor:
Lilly

Staff:

700 worldwide

Locations:

Bangkok, THAILAND

Buenos Aires, ARGENTINA

Chicago, IL

Cincinnati, OH

Dubai, UAE

Hamburg, GERMANY

Hong Kong, CHINA

Irvine, CA

Jakarta, INDONESIA

London, UK

Madrid, SPAIN

Mexico City, MEXICO

Milan, ITALY

New York, NY

Paris, FRANCE

San Francisco, CA

São Paulo, BRAZIL

Seattle, WA

Seoul, SOUTH KOREA

Shanghai, CHINA

Singapore

Stockholm, SWEDEN

Sydney, AUSTRALIA

Taipei, TAIWAN

Tokyo, JAPAN

The Firm

Landor Associates was founded in San Francisco in 1941 by industry pioneer and German expatriate Walter Landor. "Landor was ahead of his time when he set out to prove that design, when backed by consumer insight, could be a powerful identity and brand tool. Built upon his vision, Landor has a rich heritage of brand strategy and design leadership, and today has more than twenty offices in sixteen countries," says Hayes Roth, Vice President of Worldwide Marketing. Landor, the first truly international branding and design firm, has worked with a wide variety of companies all over the world, including FedEx, Microsoft, BP, France Telecom, Ford and Frito-Lay.

Landor's Breakaway Brands® philosophy differentiates them from their competitors. Their design solutions emerge from comprehensive research, analysis and strategic thinking that's focused on an individual client's needs. Although no two Landor programs are exactly alike, most are derived from a well-defined process (see page 94).

Landor's history is also unique. Walter Landor purchased the Klamath, a working ferryboat on San Francisco Bay, and turned it into Landor Associates' corporate headquarters from 1964 to 1987. In 1988, they outgrew the Klamath and moved to their current headquarters, but the current generation of Landor employees carries the creative and innovative legend of the Klamath with·them in the form of their corporate symbol, above.

Lilly

Answers That Matter.

The Client Project

Eli Lilly and Company is a global pharmaceutical company known for developing break-through drugs. In the past, Lilly was focused on communicating to health care professionals, but with the changing market their audience had grown to include consumers, recruits, investors and potential business partners. "Lilly asked Landor to determine the value of building a corporate brand and to devise a strategy for evolving Lilly from a manufacturer to a branded corporation," explains Roth.

The brand manual states that the Lilly brand represents all aspects of the global company—affiliates, therapeutic areas and functional units—and unifies them under the Lilly name. This creates a clear, coherent identity for the company.

An excerpt from the manual explains, "Answers are the essence of our brand. We provide answers through our breakthrough medicines and through the information we share. But it's more than information, it's access to knowledge and thoughtful guidance. Our new brand line—'Answers That Matter'—communicates the Lilly brand essence to the world. The Lilly Signature, our logo for more than 100 years, identifies our brand to the world. We've updated it, making it modern and personal for today's audiences. Our other core elements—color, typography, imagery, grid and rule lines—all play an important role in our proprietary look and help establish our brand character."

Lilly

Des réponses qui comptent.

Lilly

The Lilly brand line signature consists of the Lilly signature and the Lilly brand line, top. Together these two elements form the cornerstone of the corporate brand identity. The brand line has been translated into several languages, French shown above. The Lilly signature is also used alone, shown above in black.

DIN Medium
ABCDEFGHIJKLMNOPQRSTUVWXYZ
abcdefghijklmnopqrstuvwxyz
1234567890

Celeste
ABCDEFGHIJKLMNOPQRSTUVWXYZ
abcdefghijklmnopqrstuvwxyz
1234567890

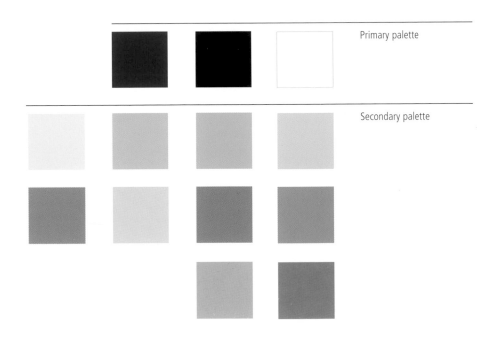

Primary palette

Secondary palette

The Brand Rules and Tools

The Lilly brand utilizes a primary type family, DIN, and a secondary family, Celeste. DIN is clean, precise and easy to read, which exemplifies Lilly's commitment to sharing information. Celeste was chosen as a serif complement to DIN and adds flexibility and variety to the system.

The preferred color application for the Lilly signature is Lilly Red. The red color conveys warmth, vitality and boldness. Black and white complete the bold, clean, primary palette. The secondary palette was developed for use throughout all the communication materials.

Photography is another powerful tool used to support and enhance the communication of the Lilly brand. The guidelines state that "it should be culturally sensitive, straightforward, modern and most of all, relevant. The use of the color red in photography further promotes our corporate color, Lilly Red." Black-and-white photography is another visually powerful option.

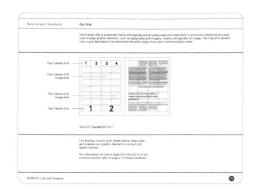

Lilly Project Team:

Margaret Youngblood, Executive Creative Director

Lori Rosenwasser, Client Director

Brad Scott, Digital Branding Director

The Lilly identity standards CD gives employees an overview of the Lilly brand essence, outlines basic graphic standards, describes the Lilly voice and the relationship of the brand elements and shows detailed examples of the brand in action. To the left are sample screens that outline the use of Lilly's grid system and show representative examples of color and black-and-white photography.

93A

Examples of Lilly communication materials before the rebranding by Landor, above.
The variety of looks and approaches is problematic and lacks clear brand definition.

The Positioning

"The previous perception of Lilly was that of a well-managed, research-oriented and trustworthy company, but not particularly differentiated from the competition. To some, Lilly was also seen to be a bit dated," explains Roth. "Creatively we were challenged to signal change in an evolutionary—rather than revolutionary—manner."

    Leveraging insight from the research, Landor developed a brand positioning for Lilly based on the concept of "answers," which encompasses both scientific answers (innovation) and questions answered (information sharing). The latter part of the positioning directly related to the research indicating that sharing information is a key manifestation of "caring."

    "This is also a positioning that was meant to extend beyond external manifestations in design and communications into the behaviors and actions of the staff and the company as a whole," says Roth.

38B-42B

The Process

Landor's process has five phases:

1) Analysis

They analyze the client's situation, industry, competition and market using visual/brand audits, management and employee interviews, research and site surveys.

2) Brand Driver™

Based on the analysis, Landor's brand consultants and designers develop various conceptual options. The Brand Driver™ is created in collaboration with the client and is a unique, compelling insight that drives and unites all aspects of brand expression.

3) Concept

The design team furthers creative development, exploring a range of creative concepts that effectively communicate the Brand Driver™ and work well on the Power Apps® applications or media that have the most power to influence brand perceptions.

4) Points of Experience

The new design system is extended to all points of brand experience and activity.

5) Realization

The branding solution is implemented across the client's products, environments or entire organization. Comprehensive guidelines help clients maintain their brand's integrity.

The Brand Look and Voice

Encompassing every touch point, Lilly's new look and feel emphasize clarity and ease of access to information. The new design system helps deliver this promise of accessibility by providing information in a straightforward, organized, visually compelling structure.

The brand voice—the verbal assets of the brand—is as important as the visual design. As the Lilly identity standards CD explains: "Every successful brand is sustained by the consistent look of its visuals and the consistent tone of its messages. The personality of our Brand Voice is that of a knowledgeable guide. Our mission is to be an ally and adviser. The intent is not to reflect the voice of our chief executive officer or any specific individual at Lilly but to represent the collective voice and values of our entire company…the resulting content is always useful, direct, brief, confident, clear and caring."

"Branding builds a specific set of expectations about our company in the minds of our audiences, creating a positive and lasting impression of Lilly."
– Lilly Identity Standards

Lilly business cards and brochures display the application of branded elements.

95A

Affiliate brochure, above right, from Sweden.
Sales aid brochure, right.

Landor put together a seven-day teaser campaign, below, that introduced the elements of the brand. The brand was launched on the eighth day and featured a video explaining the brand program and a printed mini-brand guide available in twelve languages.

The Global Brand

In creating a global brand for Lilly, Landor needed to consider the design, as well as culture, language and implementation. Each country was in charge of implementing their portion of the brand. Landor Digital Branding Director Brad Scott praises the web site implementation: "This allowed Lilly to make sure that the regulations were accurate given that region, because each region was very familiar with the way their consumers interact with prescriptions and pharmaceuticals."

Consistency was another problem that had to be overcome. Scott continues: "Until that point there were many distinct web sites. For example, the site from France had dancing Prozac pills on it. Little green and white pills doing the jig is obviously not Lilly's brand. We wanted to give people guidance. Part of that process was getting buy-ins. We conducted interviews internationally to make sure that what we were producing would actually work."

Most of Lilly's audiences don't come in contact with their business papers, so the web site becomes an extremely important conduit for information sharing. The global page, below, connects to the individual country sites, shown at bottom.

The Lilly Web Site

In addition to the new design needing to be implemented effectively for lilly.com, as well as for ten Lilly office sites around the world, the site needed to speak to a wide range of audiences—from mainstream consumers to sophisticated health care professionals.

The Landor web site elaborates: "Landor created a clean, engaging user interface design that uses a series of horizontal rules to organize information and emphasize the relevant information first. The site architecture prioritizes content from the user's perspective to create an intuitive navigation path that allows information to be accessed with ease. We produced unique, proprietary photography that supports the brand strategy. We also provided tools to enable Lilly offices around the world to adopt our design, including HTML templates, design standards and an image library."

75B

97A

Case study postcards create a compact and flexible portfolio.

Landor's own identity materials use bold color for a powerful impact, complemented by clean, organized typography.

"Anywhere you go in the world today, the work of Landor Associates is there. From airlines to financial services, telecoms to petroleum retailers, hotels to consumer products, Landor creates, builds and renews more identities and brands than any other company on earth. Linked by a worldwide digital network, our full-service offices combine the vast resources of a global design consultancy with the access and familiarity of a local partner, providing our clients with a world of expertise." —Landor Capabilities Brochure

Landor

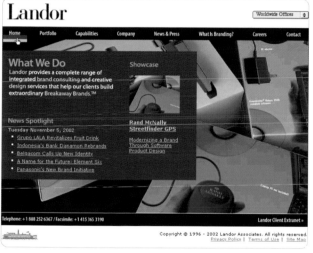

Landor's web site presents a wealth of information about the firm. The home page has rotating images that showcase various current branding solutions; a comprehensive portfolio is available for review; there is detailed information about the firm's capabilities, structure and history; and there are news, career and contact details. There is also a section that defines branding, including a useful branding dictionary and articles.

The Approach: Avoid surface treatments and discover fair, objective meanings.

Zender+Assoc:

Asbury Online

Location:

Cincinnati, OH

Principal:

P. Michael Zender

Staff:

7 professionals

The Firm

"Providing creative design excellence, serving client needs faithfully and caring for others unconditionally" is the mission of Zender + Associates. The firm was founded in 1977 by Mike Zender and Mark Eberhard at a time when there were few design firms in Cincinnati.

Over twenty-five years, the company has evolved from a design firm to an emerging agency combining media research, analysis and placement, copywriting and editing, computer programming and production with a full complement of traditional design services. Their firm overview elaborates, "Our structure allows us to serve our clients by integrating the proper mix of strategies, services, technology and solutions using both traditional and leading-edge media appropriate to their needs."

Mike Zender describes his company's philosophy: "We believe there are fair, objective meanings to be discovered. Our philosophy is still old-fashioned enough to be prescriptive, not just responsive. If you solely base your work on focus groups and what people have already experienced, you're handicapped. It's like driving down the road looking in the rearview mirror. If you carefully listen to people, filter through to their core needs and address those needs specifically, that can be really breakthrough. We like to do work where there is a very deep involvement in the content, as opposed to a surface treatment."

18B
46B-53B

ASBURY
ONLINE
INSTITUTE

nstitute

The Client Project

An excellent example of Zender's practice of providing comprehensive strategy and design services is their work for Asbury Online Institute of Pastoral Ministry (AOI), an online professional development site for pastors. AOI, a part of Asbury Theological Seminary, has a clear mission. They strive to support ministers, missionaries and Christian workers by creating an Internet-based community for lifelong learning, designed to equip for ministry in the twenty-first century.

Before working with Zender, AOI existed as an online entity—an extension of Asbury College and Asbury Theological Seminary. After a needs analysis, Zender developed a strategic marketing plan, created a new logo, redesigned the web site and produced an array of new print and web marketing materials. One of the key decisions made in response to Zender's research was that the web site cater primarily to people who were members—it would not be a marketing tool in and of itself. Other support marketing tools were created.

Also in response to the analysis, the positioning statement "Time and money...two items in short supply for busy pastors" was developed for the new AOI brand. The comprehensive marketing strategy also identified implementation tactics: "The redesign of the AOI web site will serve as the catalyst for all new marketing efforts. The message for the new look for AOI will be communicated in all channels to all AOI constituencies as much and as often as possible."

ASBURY ONLINE INSTITUTE

The new logo for Asbury Online Institute was designed to communicate both the ministry focus and digital services. Shown are the vertical version, top, and the horizontal version, above.

The Asbury Theological Seminary logo. Zender considered the context of this already-existing logo in the development of the new AOI logo, above.

101A

TRAJAN
ABCDEFGHIJKLMNOPQRSTUVWXYZ
1234567890

Officina Sans
ABCDEFGHIJKLMNOPQRSTUVWXYZ
abcdefghijklmnopqrstuvwxyz
1234567890

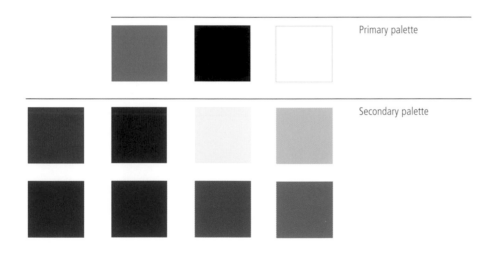

Primary palette

Secondary palette

The Brand Rules and Tools

Bold, vibrant color is a key element of the AOI brand. The color palette is uplifting and positive. Zender elaborates, "Color is a very strong identifier of the logo itself. We picked a muted blue-green for the color because it was positive. I think the color scheme really held everything together from the print to the electronic media."

Gradations and transitions from one color to another are also a key characteristic of the work. The use of gradations was intended to imply technology without being too overt a reference.

Technology influenced color choices as well. "Asbury Online Institute was primarily a web product, so we made all our color choices on the screen, then found print ink equivalents to match," explains Zender.

Also important to the print applications was the use of imagery. Subtle, large background images contrast with the smaller defined four-color photographs (see page 105A).

ASBURY ONLINE INSTITUTE

TRY AOI FREE FOR ONE QUARTER!

Just complete the information below and return this postage-paid card today!

You will find AOI
helpful for the
success of your
ministry and for
your own personal
growth – *it's a
virtual gold mine
of information*
available at no
cost to you through
this FREE trial
(a $30 value!).

31185

Name

Address

City   State   Zip

Phone (church)

Phone (home)

Email

Church

Asbury Theological Seminary Alumnus/a?   Graduation Year

For faster service, sign up at our web site, **www.aoi.edu**, *or call
1-888-AOI-0500 (1-888-264-0500) and mention this special offer!*

This reply card, which was part of the marketing program, shows one of the brand elements in action. The faded imagery of the keyboard is used in many of the applications as a background element. The repetition of the image communicates the technical nature of the client while visually connecting the pieces.

Shapes created by repeated rules are a key brand element, bringing texture and variety to the applications. These graphic elements also reflect the logo's use of gradations and rules.

Asbury Online Institute Project Team:

Mike Zender, President & Senior Designer

Nancy McIntosh, Senior Designer

Minh Troung, Staff Designer

Brian Clark, VP Marketing & Public Relations

Jerry Socha, Project Manager

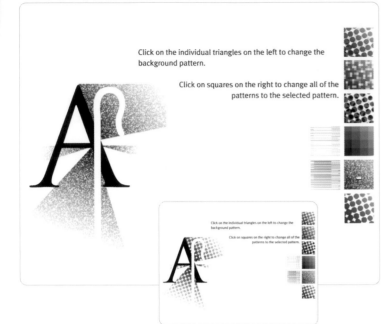

An innovative tool used during the logo development was a Flash presentation of the logo, which allowed the viewer to select from different colors and patterns, left, to explore variations.

Some of the early design explorations of the logo implied a digitized look, below. It was determined that the audience, mostly made up of "prime timers," had some aversion to high technology and were fairly conservative. This resulted in another direction, which implied technology through the use of gradation, but was not overt.

The Process

The Zender process is generally composed of five phases: needs analysis, conceptual development, design development, project production and implementation. The AOI project followed these same steps.

Prior to the rebranding, three constituencies—Asbury Seminary staff and current and former AOI members—were surveyed to help evaluate the original AOI site. The surveys asked questions about technology, usage, content preferences and future enhancements.

A complete marketing plan was developed based on the needs analysis. Three target audiences were developed: young timers (high-tech, young pastors), prime timers (low-tech, mature pastors) and globalizers (high-tech missionaries and ministers needing information anytime, anywhere).

Design development followed the marketing strategy, which clearly outlined implementation of both traditional and interactive media applications produced and distributed in three phases.

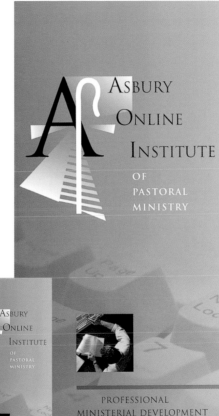

Letterhead, above, and brochure, right and bottom, show the strong use of gradations and imagery that give the print pieces a visually compelling look and feel. The tri-fold brochure was used for direct mailings and as a hand-out to distribute at conferences and seminars.

The Resulting Look

Zender describes the implementation: "The target audience turned out to be pastors in their forties and older (prime timers)—a very conservative crowd visually." Even considering this more conservative audience, Zender felt the approach of the print materials could be more visually progressive due to their strong marketing intent. These materials have a different mission from the web site, which is focused on information access and quick retrieval of content.

However, visual consistency with the web site was also very important. The applications primarily link through color use and type treatment. Zender elaborates, "The color scheme really held things together when you look from the brochure to the electronic brochure to the web site."

18B

46B-53B

105A

ASBURY
ONLINE
INSTITUTE OF PASTORAL MINISTRY

OVERVIEW
SAMPLES
PARTNER PUBLICATIONS
WHAT MEMBERS SAY
FREE TRIAL OFFER
CONTACT US
START

Introducing

The pastorate is too demanding ... serving the King too rewarding ... to ever stop learning.

Dr. Maxie Dunnam,
President
Asbury Theological Seminary

Asbury Online Institute of Pastoral Ministry

Professional ministerial development and personal growth in an online learning environment.
www.aoi.edu

Time and Money are two items in short supply for busy pastors.

What can you do to keep your skills sharp and grow spiritually at the same time?

Wouldn't it be great if you could:

Subscribe to over 80 periodicals and take time to search them for relevant ministry articles.

Regularly attend national conferences, seminary classes, lectures and forums.

Read reviews of the latest cutting-edge ministry books.

Earn continuing education credit (CEU's) at your convenience from your home or office.

Dialogue with others in the minstry from around the world.

Now you can virtually with the Asbury Online Institute (www.aoi.edu).

The Z.brochure

83B Created by Zender, a Z.brochure is "a small, stand-alone electronic brochure (meaning that it does not require separate software to run it) that is very much like a mini web site attached to an e-mail or contained on a CD-ROM. It allows you to communicate information (text, graphics and even audio) interactively like a web site but without actually being on the web."

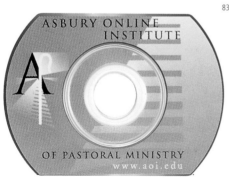

The Z.brochure designed for AOI was created both as a business card-sized CD-ROM, left, and for e-mail use. This marketing tool featured an overview of the AOI site, sample articles, an audio seminar excerpt, featured publications, testimonials, web links and an embedded registration form for free trial sign-up and collecting contact information. It was also converted into a PDF format for even greater flexibility.

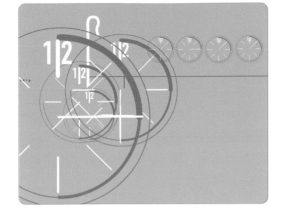

AOI's web site redesign is targeted to current members. The home page focuses on usability and information access instead of marketing, and presents a summary of recent articles. The template designed by Zender, below, shows clear hierarchy and visual organization. Their original grid structure "sketch," bottom, demonstrates their thought process.

People didn't understand the comprehensiveness and concept of the web site, so the Z.brochure was created to explain its major components and benefits. This marketing tool immediately connects the audience with an initial animation of clocks, top, and the tagline "Time and money…two items in short supply for busy pastors." The user links to introductory copy, an overview, sample articles, information about partner publications, testimonials from members, and free trial information.

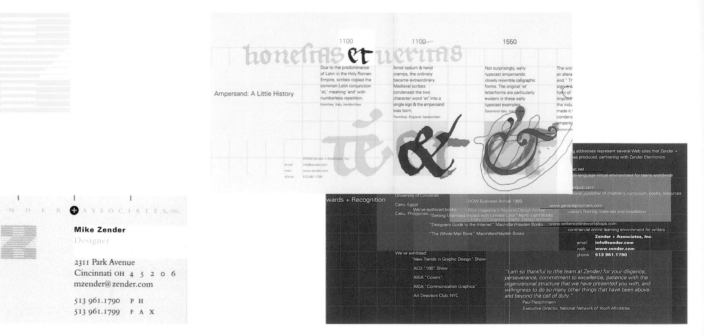

Zender + Associates business card, above.

In their innovative accordion-folded promotional brochure, a portion of the front and back are shown, right, presenting the firm's marriage of education and practice. The reader is taken on a short journey through the history of the ampersand. This cleverly connects back to the name of Zender + Associates, and to the firm's practice of teaming traditional and new media, as well as media and message.

The identity materials for Zender focus on the themes of beauty and truth, central tenets of their philosophy. According to Mike Zender, "It is our privilege at Zender + Associates to discover, create and distribute beauty…to discover, embrace and express true things… not just for ourselves but for our clients and our world. Beauty/truth is a quest; it is our gift to share."

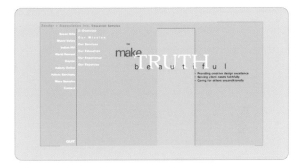

The Zender + Associates web site, above.

Zender + Associates has created several Z.brochures to promote their various services, right. These are used to market into niche areas, like educational institutions, publication design and design for youth audiences. Each of these electronic brochures follows the same format. Through color and typography they visually link to the Zender web site while maintaining a unique look.

The Approach: A diverse mix of perspectives boosts creativity.

300FeetOut

Academy of

Location:

San Francisco, CA

Principals:

Nina Dietzel

Mary Flood

Ryan Mitchell

Staff:

6 professionals

The Firm

Their web site asks the question: "300FeetOut. Out of what?" and answers: "Out of the average. Out of day-to-day life. Out of the blue. Our name doesn't make any sense, and it makes all the sense in the world: our office was 300FeetOut on historic Pier 9, over San Francisco Bay. 300FeetOut is an approach…constantly evolving, redefining communication. Moving our clients 300FeetOut of the clutter. We are YOU, to the power of 300FeetOut."

Founded in 1997, the firm is a multinational team—you're likely to hear German, Japanese, Swedish, Spanish, Indonesian, Vietnamese and Korean on any given day—whose idea is simple: "Design for every medium, equally." Nina Dietzel, President and Chief Creative Officer, elaborates, "How we implement our process differentiates us. We get a bunch of extremely creative, international people together from the beginning of the project. Teamwork, project management and customer service are all key for us."

At the core of the 300FeetOut culture are strong beliefs. Dietzel says, "Our measure of success is being able to excel without the bosses around." She adds a few guidelines they like to abide by: "Technology is here to help us—use it only if it does. Image is important—it's our business. More than anything, we believe someone is going to come through the door each morning and bring something new—something mind-blowing—to the table. So we believe in listening."

Friends

ACADEMY OF
FRIENDS

The Client Project

300FeetOut also believes in giving back and getting involved, which includes doing pro bono work for organizations like Academy of Friends (AOF). Senior Art Director Ryan Mitchell describes their client: "AOF was founded in 1980 as a small, private Oscar Night party. Over subsequent parties, the gala became an HIV/AIDS fundraiser, reaction to the toll HIV was taking on the community. Today, Academy of Friends and its annual gala is the largest Oscar Night party outside of L.A. and one of the largest contributors to Bay Area HIV/AIDS organizations…to date raising over four million dollars."

AOF came to 300FeetOut to produce an integrated print and web campaign for the 2002 Gala. This involved a new identity and stationery system, advertisements, invitations, outdoor billboards, event tickets, event signage and a redesigned web site. Mitchell continues, "The communication goals were to present a re-energized, top-notch organization through a rebranding and to establish the Academy of Friends Gala as the fundraising event of the year."

18B

46B-53B

A deflated San Francisco economy and subsequent effects of September 11 left fundraising dollars difficult to come by. We knew that more attention would need to be focused on enticing underwriters than ever before." These factors changed the focus of the project implementation, and it worked. The event attracted an enormous crowd and proved to be very successful.

Primary logo lock-up, top.
Secondary lock-up, above.

Previous AOF logo.

111A

ITC Avant Garde Gothic
ABCDEFGHIJKLMNOPQRSTUVWXYZ
abcdefghijklmnopqrstuvwxyz
1234567890

Interstate
ABCDEFGHIJKLMNOPQRSTUVWXYZ
abcdefghijklmnopqrstuvwxyz
1234567890

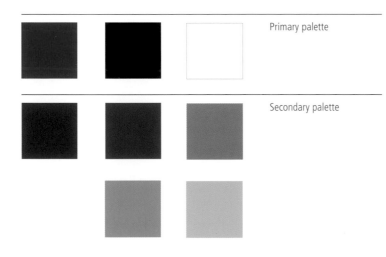

Primary palette

Secondary palette

The Brand Rules and Tools

Mitchell describes the team's design intent: "The strategy behind the campaign came mostly as a reaction to what had been done unsuccessfully in the past. Previous campaigns had been timid and bland. We knew we wanted to go in exactly the opposite direction."

Their choice of fonts reflects this direction. "ITC Avant Garde Gothic was chosen as the logotype font because of its visual connection to the ribbon/filmstrip bug. The point of the *R* is reflected in the sharpness of the ribbon, the roundness of the *C* and *O* reflect the loop of the bug, and the vertical appearance of *Friends* reflects the same in the ribbon/filmstrip. Interstate was chosen as a secondary font for its ease of readability and its more vertical appearance." A weighty event logotype, right, was developed, using Interstate, to add consistency and clarity to the applications.

Academy of Friends Project Team:

Nina Dietzel, Creative Director

Ryan Mitchell, Senior Art Director

Mary Flood, Senior Producer

Alexander Grossman, Copywriter

Robert Bengston, Photographer

The bold, simple color palette also brought visual strength and meaning to the solution. Mitchell continues, "The use of red came as a way of linking the palettes of the AIDS ribbon and the regal runway of the Oscars® and provided a striking backdrop for the various design pieces. With billboards, bus shelters, posters and invitations plastering the city…our campaign literally left the 'town painted red'."

The secondary palette used on applications such as the postcards was chosen to create a rich and glamorous look and feel. Dark brown, copper, silver, deep blue and burnt orange all complement the strong primary palette to convey the glitz and glamour of the event.

22ND ANNUAL ACADEMYOF FRIENDS GALA SUNDAY MARCH24

The logotype developed for the gala, above, was used consistently throughout all the applications.

113A

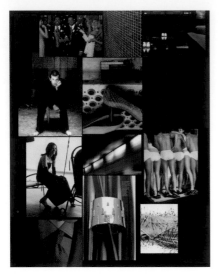

Concept mood board.

The five logos, far right, were presented to the board of directors for final selection:
From the top, right:
1 Combination of the AIDS ribbon and a piece of film (developed into final).
2 A play on the Oscar figure, also representing the volunteers—a figure of hope.
3 A supportive and nurturing relationship is symbolized through the flame of hope.
4 The typography symbolizes the coming together of people and services in support of the cause.
5 The diverse letterforms of *A, O,* and *F* symbolize the diverse people that unite to make the event possible and the diverse group of people that benefit from the cause.

The Process

Mitchell describes the process: "This project presented a unique situation with an approval board of directors committee of over twenty-five people. A considerable amount of education was needed in order to get everyone on the same page. Identity was naturally the first item addressed. 18B Designs and conceptual descriptions were posted to an online project management site to allow everyone interested the opportunity to comment." Mood boards, left, were then created to establish the base design direction to all other aspects of the campaign. These concepts were reviewed via the project management site before the final selection was made.

It was important to the project team to communicate that the event, rather than being exclusive, was a night open to anyone interested in the fight against HIV/AIDS.

As is often the case with nonprofits, 300FeetOut had to walk a delicate line between creating compelling materials speaking to a sophisticated audience and creating excessive or wasteful materials. The team created high-quality work while cutting costs by using existing photography and having a great relationship with a local printer.

ACADEMY *of*
FRIENDS

Invitations and a "Save the Date" card were some of the first materials received by event patrons.

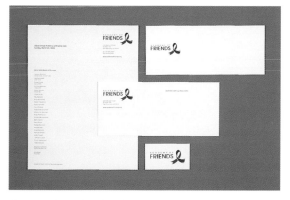

The project began by rebranding the core organization, including a new logo and new stationery package.

The Resulting Look

After living and breathing Academy of Friends for nearly a year, the collection and range of promotional materials developed by 300FeetOut was impressive. The team handled almost every aspect of the campaign, resulting in an extremely cohesive, bold, sophisticated package for the gala.

Limited imagery in key areas and applications compliments the strong use of color and shape. "The main approach, with the imagery, was to bump up the saturation of the images or to present them as duotone images, both for the purpose of creating a rich and seductive look and feel," explains Mitchell.

In these postcards, as with many of the applications,
copywriting played a key role in the concept execution.

The use of outdoor advertising was key to getting the word out. The 300FeetOut
team actually used fewer outdoor spaces for the big billboards than in previous years. Yet
given the strong use of color, the impact was powerful, and the message was clearly visible.

Color was the greatest link between all the print and web applications. In addition,
the large, punchy headlines, the gala logotype and the AOF logo created a strong bond
between all the applications.

Outdoor advertising—bus shelters, above, and billboards, top right—was an important aspect of promoting the event to a broad audience.

How to make print interactive:
Consider the audience. Use all the tools available.
Important messages come first. Have fun with the details.
Think beyond the immediate project.
–www.300feetout.com

Promotional postcards packaged together with a black paper band, top. Color was used to code the various tickets for the event and to bring visual variety to the collection, above.

The Web Site

Mitchell explains his thoughts about the web site: "Having been to the gala for the first time last year, I was awestruck by the sheer magnitude of the event and the scale of it all. I would have loved to convey this scale throughout the web site by showcasing large event images on all the landing pages. Unfortunately large images make for very heavy pages and slow load time, so the sacrifice was made to showcase only one awe-inspiring image on the home page and to use large typography instead on secondary pages to help convey this message."

The AOF web site.

identity

The moving card 300FeetOut used when they moved from the pier to their present location.

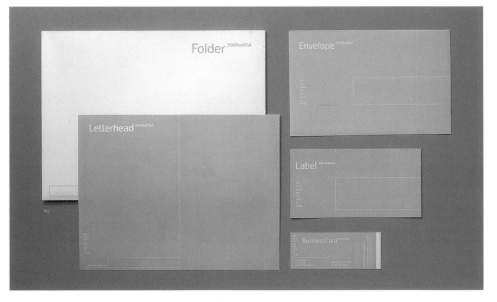

300FeetOut's stationery uses typography and unusual formats to emphasize their clever approach.

"What separates us from the competition is our dedication to process…making sure it works, and it works for everyone. We have a robust intranet. We keep our schedules, deliverables and current updates there. We keep work online for our clients' convenience and our own sanity and we don't run with scissors." –www.300feetout.com

300FeetOut

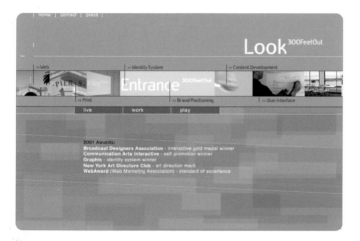

Typography and color visually integrate the identity. The web site uses a moving band of images to bring variety and interest throughout the pages. The site features a portfolio page; information about the firm, including culture, history and management pages; detailed case studies (featuring client pop-up pages); lists of clients and services; and a fun "toys" page, which allows download of various (very cool) screen savers.

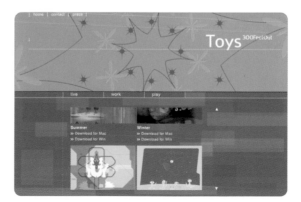

119A

The Approach: Work with a 360-degree approach to brand development.

VSA Partners

Baker

Locations:

Chicago, IL

New York, NY

Principals:

Dana Arnett

Kerry Kitch

Jamie Koval

Curt Schreiber

Jeff Walker

Staff:

Chicago: 60

New York: 5

KOVAL

The Firm

Established in 1982, VSA Partners has an international reputation for creating large-scale, complex branding solutions. The firm's work has created an impression in the marketplace for such brands as Cingular, Harley-Davidson and IBM. After starting off in graphic design, VSA began developing and influencing the course of brands almost inadvertently: clients who valued the firm's strategic thinking, design depth and executional abilities increasingly invited the firm to reposition or launch their brands. Today, brand development is a core competency at VSA, stemming directly from a deep understanding of a client's executive vision, corporate culture, product and service offerings.

Principal Jamie Koval says, "To VSA, a brand is a tool for making and fulfilling a promise to an audience. It's a belief that reverberates throughout an organization, from the way it presents its visual identity, to its online presence, to the way its employees answer the phone." This broad perspective on brand requires both detailed analysis and a broad integration of resources to create meaningful brand experiences. VSA works from the inside 54B ⊙ out—building a foundation on the realities and potential of an organization—to shape how a client is seen, how its products or services are positioned, and how its customers interact with and experience its brand. This 360-degree approach explains why VSA's staff comprises strategists, designers, information architects, writers, technologists, researchers and account managers.

The Client Project

Baker Furniture selected VSA Partners to redefine and reposition its brand within the residential furniture industry. Baker, owned by Kohler, is an almost century-old company with an extraordinary legacy of craftsmanship and design in luxury home furnishings. The Baker web site recalls the company roots: "At the beginning, Siebe Baker worked with his hands. Later, the success of his sturdy furniture allowed his son, Hollis Baker, to study at university, travel the Old World and hone the eye of a collector. Today these two thoughts, the eye and the hand, remain the cornerstone of Baker Furniture."

Baker came to VSA for two primary reasons. First, their customer base and competition were changing, and secondly, they simply wanted a change. Initially, as Koval recalls, Baker viewed their issue as basically an advertising problem. "Although we felt their advertising could be more effective, we believed that their challenges were deeper than a new campaign. We felt there was an opportunity to take a holistic approach to Baker's communication efforts," he says. "Our first step was to help them understand how to align all their marketing communications under one voice." To help illustrate this approach, the VSA team presented Baker an extended campaign including advertising, web, retail environments, catalogs, direct mail and proprietary publications. Key to the campaign was qualitative research. The project team discovered through focus group testing that Baker needed to rejuvenate its demographic, making itself more relevant to the younger, affluent consumer. Timeless integrity and relevance remained central to the concept.

⊙ 69B

VSA consolidated all of Baker's brands under one identity to ensure that their word mark is always consistent throughout every channel.

121A

Adobe Garamond
ABCDEFGHIJKLMNOPQRSTUVWXYZ
abcdefghijklmnopqrstuvwxyz
1234567890

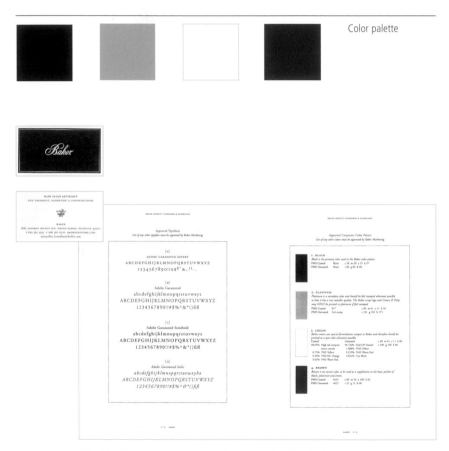

Color palette

Baker identity guide sample spread, above. Baker Furniture business card front and back, above left. Baker brand design and typography is characterized by clarity and sensitivity.

The Brand Rules and Tools

VSA recommended Baker abandon its corporate colors of dark green and gold because they felt dated and too conservative. Black, platinum and cream became the new standard. Black is the primary color in the Baker palette, communicating a sensibility of design clarity, simplicity and sophistication. Platinum is foil-stamped whenever possible to convey quality and cream gives a sense of warmth. Brown is an accent color, employed as a supplement to the primary palette.

VSA also developed new typographic standards for a level of refinement and consistency. The brand typography is set in the Adobe Garamond family—its elegance is a thoughtful match for the Baker aesthetic and effectively communicates the company's history, quality and attention to detail. To make Baker products more aspirational, lifestyle black-and-white photography plays an important role, both as a brand element and in differentiating Baker communications in a crowded, colorful, competitive environment. These photographs communicate as much about

64B

lifestyle as they do about the product, showing tightly cropped figures interacting with furniture. These visual elements present a clear departure from the past and establish a more progressive, consumer-focused direction for the company.

VSA's communication platform for Baker addresses three distinct audiences—interior designers; independent furniture dealers, such as Marshall Field's; and end-users—each with their own expectations of Baker and each with their own roles in a purchasing decision. The use of a variety of photographic types (see page 126A) works well to bring variety to the work, as well as to consistently bridge communication expectations of all target audiences.

Baker Project Team:

Jamie Koval, Creative Director

Dan Knuckey, Design Director

Brock Conrad, Designer

Katie Heit, Designer

Anne Zagotta, Account Director

Melissa McManamy, Account Manager

Andy Blankenburg, Writer

Baker

Haven *from* Barbara Barry

FURNITURE · FABRIC · ACCESSORIES AVAILABLE TO DESIGNERS AT BAKER SHOWROOMS FOR THE NEAREST LOCATION VISIT BAKERFURNITURE.COM OR CALL 1 800 59 BAKER

Black-and-white photography is used in advertising, catalogs, web site and other promotional materials to differentiate the brand from the competition, focus the viewer's attention on the form of the furniture and communicate an attitude of sophisticated simplicity.

123A

20B-23B

Baker 2002 national ad library CD, top.
Baker upholstery sale postcard, above.

"You can change
market perceptions by placing
an existing identity in a new context
—applying it in an innovative way
that audiences still
recognize as authentic."
–James Koval

The Process

While every brand challenge is unique, VSA works from a consistent framework to develop, execute and evaluate its solutions. VSA sets priorities through their approach, specifically asking the question, "What do you want to achieve?" before answering, "How should you look and sound?" This approach consists of five steps:

1. Frame: Define the business problem early and concisely. Set the program's strategic direction, goals and objectives. Scope, research, plan and structure the program elements.

2. Concept: Strategize on how to formulate, extend or apply a brand to differentiate an organization or offering in its competitive environment. Define the value offered, find unique strengths, capture "voice," identify media, build consensus, plan to operationalize.

3. Create: Bring the assignment to life. Shape the communications around a sustainable brand. Define a standard. Explore multiple directions, evaluate potential, determine elements. Map out execution, sequencing and measurement.

4. Implement: Execute the plan and engage the audience. Operationalize the brand. Produce the elements: web development, programming, print production, training, events. Monitor and manage actively. Respond to opportunities. Deliver as promised.

5. Validate: Did we hit the target? Did we move the needle? Do people believe? Do they behave differently? Did the client profit? Do we need to make adjustments? Did the work redefine a product? A service? An organization? An entire industry?

For Baker, as for all clients, the teams at VSA are client-centric rather than defined by function or hierarchy. "We don't have a clear-cut web group, an account group or a design group," explains Jamie Koval. "Teams are built based on specific clients' needs or objectives. We pair different disciplines together to collaborate on an assignment. It encourages key learning, but more importantly, it's essential in obtaining great results." Built into VSA's process is its "agency report card." This added step gives VSA and its clients the opportunity to critique each other following key milestones.

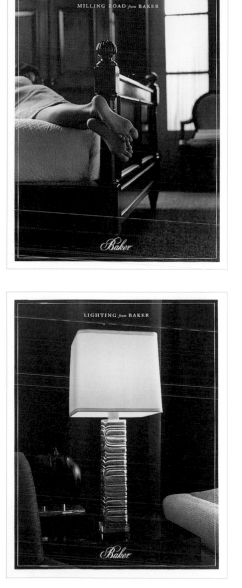

The Lasting Result

The program VSA established for Baker grew in scope to become comprehensive. VSA crafted Baker's brand positioning and shored up its visual identity. They redesigned and relaunched Baker's web site, adding richer levels of content, improving the user experience and a design that is a true extension of the brand. They articulated Baker's "guiding principles" for internal audiences. They redesigned Baker's system of catalogs, and national and dealer advertising. VSA also created signage for the retail stores and showrooms, as well as supporting promotional materials.

71B

Collection catalog covers, clockwise starting top left: Milling Road, Thomas Pheasant, Haven from Barbara Barry, and Lighting.

PROCESS TIP

For Baker's pitch presentation, VSA showed advertisements from eight furniture companies with logos removed. This clearly and visually made their point that the companies could not be differentiated—their approaches were all too similar. It also helped the client's comfort level with the new approach.

64B

Baker's Haven from Barbara Barry catalog shows the variety of photographic types, from full-bleed photographs to outlines and details.

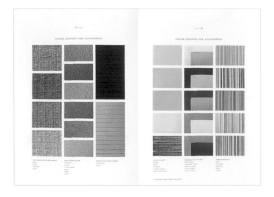

Again, says Koval, the operative word is alignment. "We work closely with organizations to help them see their employees as an extension of their brand. That single step often can be more powerful than anything you can do from an external marketing standpoint." The materials produced for Baker, says Koval, feel more relevant and are more focused on capturing the Baker lifestyle. "It's very much about articulating the connection between the individual and the product. It's meant to be very intimate, well designed and elegant. If anything, it probably falls more in line with fashion than furniture, which tends to connote a feeling more than a written message. It's intentionally very open-ended."

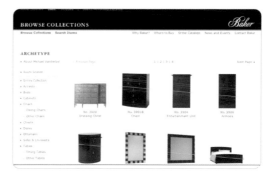

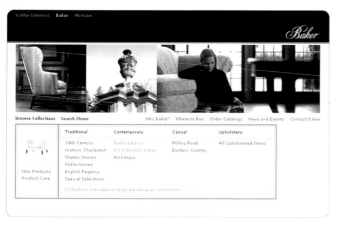

The Web Site

The site effectively showcases the collections and offers the lifestyle and product specifications needed by end users and designers. It also provides invaluable background information about the company, giving the audience a true appreciation for the heritage and quality behind the Baker name.

75B

Baker web site home page, above left, and the pages for one of the collections, above.

identity

VSA's web site is a microcosm of the firm's philosophy, capabilities and wit. Speaking to

54B ◎ the prospective client, it says: "What we offer you is a group of intelligent and highly caffeinated problem solvers who would like nothing more than to help you figure out how to use the Internet, print and traditional media to improve your company's unique position in the marketplace....The main thing we offer is a holistic look at your brand that connects it all and shows itself (in a good way) on your bottom line."

VSA Partners promotional book.

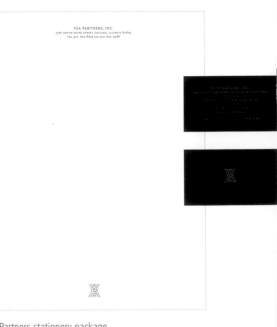

VSA Partners stationery package.

We are a strategic design and branding consultancy.

VSA's web site home page, above; one of several profile pages, right; and process page, below right. The thoughtful addition of sound and animation integrate with the visuals to clarify and intensify the site's communication.

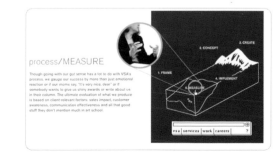

"We are the nagging stepsisters of brand identity,
constantly asking,
'You're not really going to wear that, are you?'"
– www.vsapartners.com

The Approach: Work from the inside out for powerful design impact.

Leonhardt:Fitch
RMW

Location:

Seattle, WA

Principals:

Sue Nixon

Ray Ueno

Tracy Wald

Staff:

40 professionals

The Firm

"At Leonhardt:Fitch we've come to believe that the design impact is at its most powerful when it works from the inside out. When it's viewed internally as the essential proof of the unification of the organization around a common purpose. Design, through the application of craft and attention to detail, reinforces the belief that each employee has a common shared set of values and principles. When every member of an organization buys into the brand message, you have the basis for a very strong, long-lasting brand," explains founder Ted Leonhardt.

Based in Seattle, the firm was originally founded by Ted and Carol Leonhardt over twenty-five years ago. The company is now a part of the Fitch Network, owned by Cordiant Communications, which includes approximately thirty design communications companies internationally. Leonhardt:Fitch has internal teams composed of design, strategy, account management, programming, video, production and management.

20B-23B

President and CEO Sue Nixon speaks about the firm's pragmatic approach to branding: "We have seven steps to partnering with clients in today's market: 1. understanding the implications of change; 2. including the right decision makers; 3. agreeing on the objectives; 4. forcing alignment and sharing ownership; 5. executing the details; 6. measuring results where possible; and 7. leveraging experience and learning from the process."

vision
function
space
culture
ideas
experience

RMW think
listen
build
speak
learn

architecture & interiors

The Client Project

Leonhardt:Fitch's work for RMW Architecture & Interiors is a great example of this partnering approach. RMW's overview brochure explains their philosophy: "Speak ideas, think space, build culture. Design is a conversation between people, environment and culture. The quality of the end result is often a result of the quality of the conversation. Architecture and interiors are dialogues. Back-and-forth paths that lead somewhere new....We build enduring and meaningful places for people to live and work and come together as communities."

RMW was founded in 1970 and has grown to a staff of over one hundred. Sue Nixon says, "We began working with RMW in 2000 after a year-long selection process. They were in the midst of internal change to a group structure with multiple offices. Our assignment required that we develop a new visual/verbal language that reflected their changing culture and new perspective. We developed a look and feel for the RMW brand that is infused with the spirit of architecture and defining spaces and captures the cerebral process RMW employs when designing them. The work covered all aspects: brand development, identity, print, web, interactive presentation and ongoing consulting."

The new RMW logo is composed of three parts: logotype, "contextual modifiers" and "identifier" (describing the services of "architecture & interiors"). All three elements bring meaning to the brand.

experience
RMW think

architecture & interiors

RMW primary logo, top.
Secondary logo in one color, above. The "contextual modifiers" are reduced from eleven to two words when space becomes an issue.

Previous RMW logo.

Trade Gothic
ABCDEFGHIJKLMNOPQRSTUVWXYZ
abcdefghijklimnoqrstuvwxyz
1234567890

Trade Gothic Italic
ABCDEFGHIJKLMNOPQRSTUVWXYZ
abcdefghijklimnoqrstuvwxyz
1234567890

Trade Gothic Bold Two
ABCDEFGHIJKLMNOPQRSTUVWXYZ
abcdefghijklmnopqrstuvwxyz
1234567890

Primary palette

The Brand Rules and Tools

The RMW brand guide outlines the use of typography and color. "Clean, sophisticated and approachable, Trade Gothic is the primary typeface." The various weights of roman and italic are used for text, headlines and callouts.

The primary colors for the brand are RMW Gray and RMW Green. The gray is Pantone 8600, metallic gray. When metallic inks are not possible, an alternative dark gray is specified. The green, Pantone 390, is a very contemporary and intense color that contrasts the neutral gray. In the print collateral, the green is used in smaller quantities, as a highlight color, to call out important information. Blue is used, primarily in the web applications, as a secondary color. This color is also found in much of the color architectural photography.

Other visual characteristics of the applications are a strong use of white space and progressive typography.

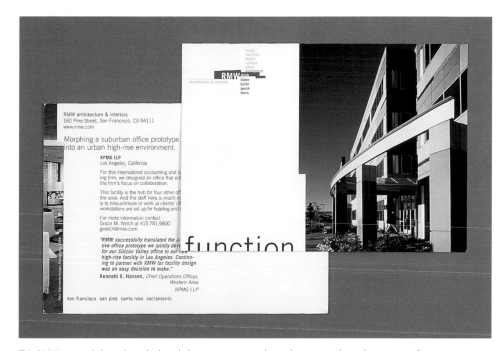

This RMW postcard shows how the brand elements come together: color, typography and strong use of photography and white space. These postcards are used to highlight specific RMW projects.

"RMW is seen as a group of great people with a strong culture and values creating powerful design that impacts people and enhances business."
—John Close

RMW Project Team:

John Close, Designer

Ron Sasaki, Account Services Manager

Lori Mahoney, Electronic Production

Ali Weeks, Designer

Lesley Wikoff, Designer

Jackie Wanaka, Print Production

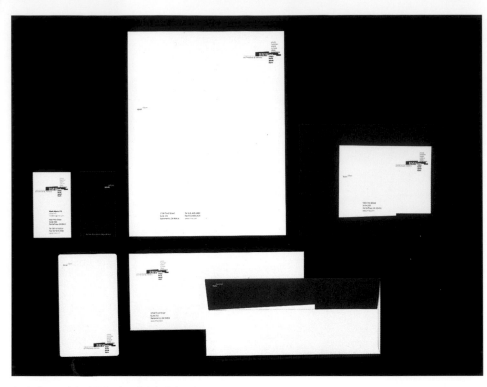

At the heart of the RMW rebranding is their stationery identity. Strong contrast between the large areas of white and the dark gray shapes gives the stationery components structure and drama.

20B-23B

The Process

John Close, creative director and lead designer for the RMW project, describes Leonhardt:Fitch's process: "Our projects start with an analysis of the client, audience, issues and points of difference. There is an initial process of information gathering and interviews which results in a hardworking document about the client's heritage, personality, tone, services and emotional connection to their audience. Then the design team takes that target and goes forth with design."

He continues, "For RMW, the strategy team took the lead driving the front end and analyzing the current name and competitive set. There was a point of handoff where the strategy group made their recommendations, marking the kickoff of the creative process. As the lead designer, I was involved from the beginning, but at that point I guided the process. An account manager was present through the entire project to mind the details and make sure everything was moving."

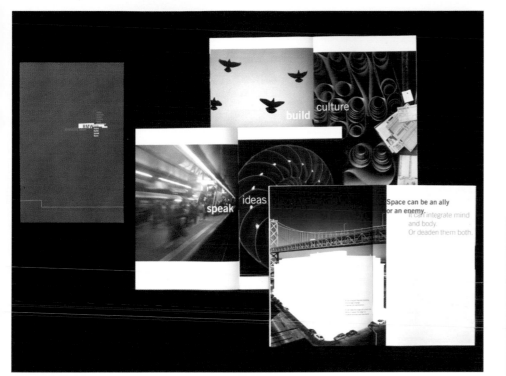

The Resulting Look

It became obvious in the early stages of the analysis that RMW was known for their strong client relationships, the quality of their staff, and their practicality and professionalism. Unfortunately, this perception lacked an understanding of their passion for design. It was important for the design team to emphasize RMW's thoughtfulness, energy and innovation. Close elaborates, "The contextual modifiers of 'think, listen, build, speak and learn' became the foundations of the brand. The impact, at the end of the day, is the 'vision, function, space, culture, ideas and experience.' They want to be able to tell their story consistently and effectively, and they want it to be about the client and the impact."

Their introductory brochure is a very thought-provoking, conceptual overview piece, shown above, which discusses the relationship between people and spaces. It is a compelling statement about design's impact on business and people.

RMW's overview brochure, above left, is used as an introductory piece to prospective clients. It speaks to their philosophy and highlights their unique perspective on architecture and design.

RMW used the card above to announce their thirtieth anniversary. This piece also introduced and reinforced the new brand.

135A

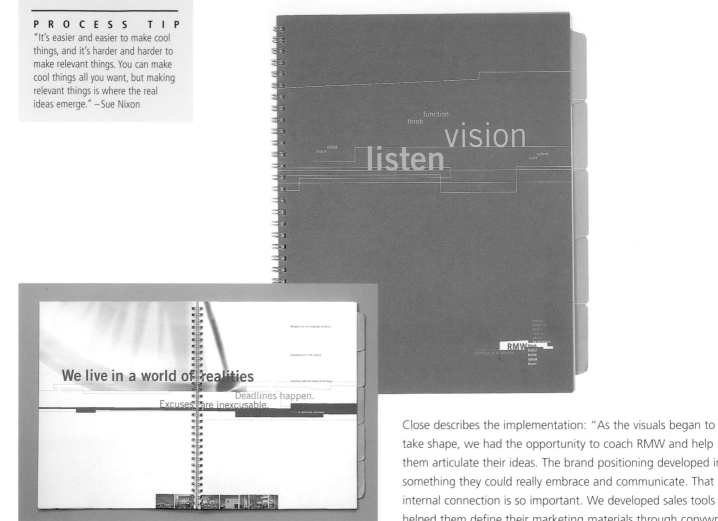

RMW capabilities brochure inside spread and cover.

Close describes the implementation: "As the visuals began to take shape, we had the opportunity to coach RMW and help them articulate their ideas. The brand positioning developed into something they could really embrace and communicate. That internal connection is so important. We developed sales tools and helped them define their marketing materials through copywriting and design, things that really helped them develop a vocabulary. This allowed them to ultimately elevate their conversations with their clients to the level of their passion and philosophy."

The Web Site

RMW had a progressive vision for the web. Because the site is targeted to a specialized audience, they wanted the experience to elevate the overall concept. With the web came the opportunity to bring in movement, a sense of space and the integration of language.

"The web site clearly demonstrates the special point of view of a design-driven organization that sees its brand and the resulting visual identity as a reflection of core beliefs and principles," reflects Leonhardt.

75B

The web site splash page, above left, home page, top, people page, middle, and specific project description page, bottom.

identity

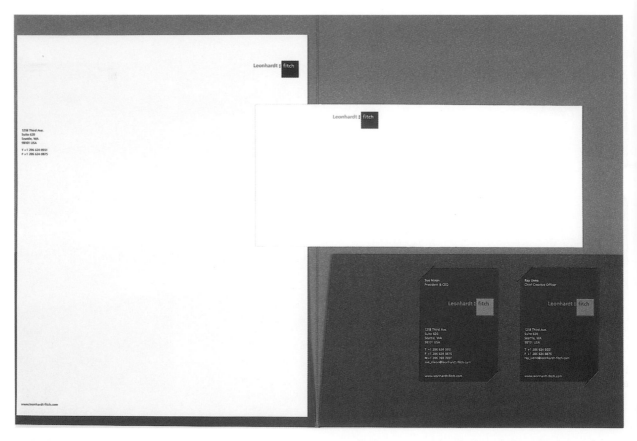

Leonhardt:Fitch's stationery package.

Formerly The Leonhardt Group, Leonhardt:Fitch was originally founded on the principle that great design is created using a team approach. Another founding principle was that design should be grounded in solid business strategy. Even with the growth and expansion of the firm, this philosophy continues to guide them today.

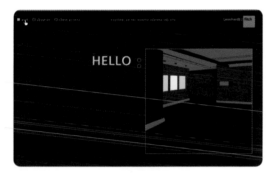

Leonhardt : fitch

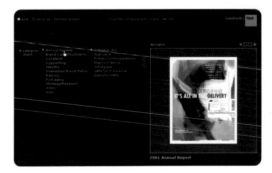

Leonhardt:Fitch's web site uses striking, clean illustrations and a palette of gray, black and highlighting colors to communicate a clear message. Information about the principals, above, and a comprehensive portfolio, right, are at the heart of the site content.

"People want to be hopeful. They want to trust, so the more authentic the message can be, the more likely they will settle into it."
— Sue Nixon

139A

The Approach: Empower your employees so creativity can thrive.

VMA:
Cincinnat

Location:
Dayton, OH

Principals:
Kenneth Botts
Greg Fehrenbach
Steve Goubeaux
Joel Warneke

Staff:
13 professionals

The Firm

Engage. Enliven. Enlighten. Enrich. That's the philosophy behind a midsized multidisciplinary design firm in Dayton, Ohio. Visual Marketing Associates (VMA) was founded in 1985 by designer Ken Botts. He brought on a partner, Steve Goubeaux, in 1993. As Botts describes, "Steve was a great addition. He had a sales and marketing background in addition to product development, and that complemented my graphic design background. We merged in 2001 with Design Orange, a two-person design firm from Cincinnati. With the addition of Joel Warneke and Greg Fehrenbach, we now have four principals."

54B ◎
69B ◎
     From a philosophical standpoint, VMA started out as a "design plus marketing" firm. Today it's not a revolutionary idea, but in the mid-eighties few firms were thinking so holistically. "We do extensive market research. We'll test product concepts and get feedback from the end users and alter our end product to make sure that it not only meets the manufacturer's criteria but also meets the consumers' criteria."

As technology has grown and changed, so has VMA. Their three core design disciplines are graphic, digital and industrial design. As Botts continues, "Our niche is using the three disciplines to help our client partners develop product, introduce it to the trade and sell through to the consumer. We do a lot of work in the retail sectors, specifically in lifestyle-oriented product design."

Ballet

CINCINNATI *Ballet*

The Client Project

The rebranding of the Cincinnati Ballet Company represents VMA's concern for and interest in the arts. The Cincinnati Ballet is a nonprofit arts organization that has attracted some of the most talented dancers and choreographers from around the world. VMA had been working on small pro bono projects with the Ballet for two years prior to their charge to revitalize the entire look and positioning of the organization. For this large project, VMA worked on a partial pro bono/partial paid basis and designed the 2002–2003 season campaign marketing materials, web site and redesign of the corporate and academy identities.

Joel Warneke describes the project's communications goals: "We were to re-brand and reposition the company with a consistent message of world-class classical and contemporary dance, communicating the diversity of the company's performance capabilities. It was also important for us to call attention to the fortieth anniversary of the company. We wanted to celebrate this key anniversary by romantically acknowledging the past, balanced with an eye toward the future."

Through the use of unique imagery, VMA's goal was to reach the Ballet's current demographic as well as appeal to the yet untapped markets of young professionals. In addition, the imagery and specific photographic style emphasized the physicality and athleticism of the dancers as well as the aesthetics of the form and posture of the body.

THE OTTO M. BUDIG ACADEMY OF
CINCINNATI *Ballet*

Logotype for the Cincinnati Ballet, top, in blue. Logotype for the Ballet's Academy, above, in red. The mark for the Ballet, above in blue, and the Academy, in red.

CINCINNATI
Ballet

Previous logo for the Cincinnati Ballet.

POETICA ROMAN
ABCDEFGHIJKLMNOPQRSTUVWXYZ
ABCDEFGHIJKLMNOPQRSTUVWXYZ
1234567890

Rotis Semi Serif
ABCDEFGHIJKLMNOPQRSTUVWXYZ
abcdefghijklmnopqrstuvwxyz
1234567890

Rotis San Serif
ABCDEFGHIJKLMNOPQRSTUVWXYZ
abcdefghijklmnopqrstuvwxyz
1234567890

Ultra Condensed Sans One
ABCDEFGHIJKLMNOPQRSTUVWXYZ
ABCDEFGHIJKLMNOPQRSTUVWXYZ
1234567890

Ultra Condensed Serif
ABCDEFGHIJKLMNOPQRSTUVWXYZ
abcdefghijklmnopqrstuvwxyz
1234567890

The Brand Rules and Tools

Imagery, typography and color come together to create a compelling brand experience. Poetica Roman was used in the logotype and stationery package, creating a classical, graceful feel. Ultra Condensed Sans One and Ultra Condensed Serif were used for the titles on print and web applications. Warneke elaborates, "They were chosen because of their clean, contemporary look and the serif and sans serif typefaces work well together when mixed. We wanted to use a condensed font because some of the titles were lengthy and we could use it in large point sizes without it becoming overwhelming. Rotis was used for the body copy. It was also used because of its contemporary look, but more importantly, the ease of readability and its versatility."

A blue color, Pantone 647, and Pantone black were used to identify the Ballet Company's corporate side. A red, Pantone 187, and Pantone black worked in parallel for the Ballet's Academy. The red and blue "color coding" is used in the

Primary colors
Corporate

Primary colors
Academy

mark and logotype developed for both (see page 141). The corporate mark is always used on its own and never locked up with the logotype.

The other main design element that separates the corporate identity from the Academy identity is the image of the outstretched ballerina. The Academy version incorporates an image of a young girl, lower right, emulating the position of the professional dancer, right, used in the corporate materials.

An anniversary mark was created for use during the 2002–2003 season.

Business card, below, showing the relationship between the imagery, logo and typography.

Cincinnati Ballet Project Team:

Rob Anspach, Production Design

Ken Botts, Project Management

Greg Fehrenbach, Account Management

Jeff Goeke, Graphic Design

Patrick Jennings, Photography

Jef Mayer, Digital Design

Tom McMenamin, Digital Design Management

Joel Warneke, Graphic Design &
 Creative Design Direction

Logo explorations.

The Process

VMA's basic process breaks down into four main categories: research design, creative design, production design, and reproduction design. Ken Botts describes the process for the Cincinnati Ballet project: "The design team consisted of a principal to oversee the account management, creative director for brand management, graphic designer and production designer for the execution of the print materials and an interactive designer for development of the web site. After a team meeting with the client/partner to determine marketing objectives, the print design team members took the lead to generate the new logo and application to the stationery system. After initial concepts were generated for several of the print brochures and posters, the digital design team members began to interpret key design elements to develop a parallel web site."

20B-23B

Botts continues describing VMA's general teamwork philosophy: "When a project comes in, we assign a team and pick a team leader. We try to include one member for each discipline. If the project tends to be more heavily focused on interactive design, we would pick one of our digital designers to be the team leader. The team leader is the 'boss' for that project. This means our organization doesn't have the traditional hierarchy of titles because you may have several different bosses on the same day if you have more than one project. It's worked out nicely because it gives people empowerment and variety, which seems to make the creative process thrive. The more variety you have the less frequently you get stale."

Generally, one of the four partners is involved from a more global perspective, but the daily flow is controlled by the team leader. He or she is responsible for making sure all the client and marketing objectives and parameters are met.

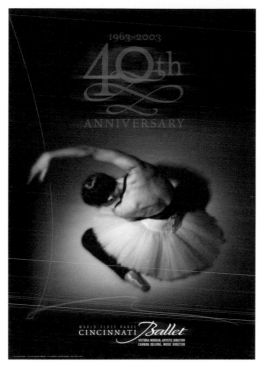

Season brochure cover, below left, and interior spread, below right.

Poster celebrating the 40th anniversary season, above. Poster kiosk, above left, outside the home of the Cincinnati Ballet Company, the Aronoff Center.

The Implementation

Photographic imagery plays a key role in the implementation and communication of the brand. Warneke describes working with the photographer: "Patrick Jennings' photographic style was perfect for what we were trying to achieve. He captured a gritty yet tasteful quality that really hasn't been seen before in promoting this art form. Through our research phase we referenced a lot of highly polished, staged and posed dance images. We wanted something a bit more personal, theatrical and unexpected, and that's exactly what Patrick captured. The duotones for the images were based on and relate to the mood or emotions you might feel during the performance."

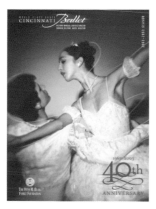

The banner for the performance of *Carmina Burana*, in context in the lobby of the Aronoff Center, above, and a process design, right.

Each performance for the season was captured in a specific color, as seen in the banner and postcard examples below. These color duotones were carried through from the print to the web applications, providing a strong color identification for the individual performance run as well as a wonderful color palette for the entire season.

Warneke speaks about one of the design team's creative challenges: "I think the biggest challenge stems from this being (for the most part) pro-bono work. Firms are only willing to give their work away for a season, maybe two. When a new firm comes in, they generally have their own creative objectives in mind. So, the brand falls by the wayside and the company's message gets lost in the shuffle from one firm to the next. I think when working pro bono, or even for compensation, designers have to remember that the creative phase is only one part of the process. Clearly and consistently communicating your client's brand and message is paramount. I do not see any reason why both objectives, creativity and consistency, can't be accomplished."

A postcard series complemented the other promotional applications. Four of the eight produced are shown left to right: *The Sleeping Beauty, Come Together Festival, Beauty and the Beast,* and *Ballet Russe de Monte Carlo.*

DESIGN TIP
"When we do three-dimensional work, I really push all of us to output a proof and assemble it—put it into context. When you are designing a 36-inch, six-sided box on a flat screen it is a different experience. In this context, we try to use the old-fashioned, hand approaches as much as we can." –Ken Botts

Sample screens from the Cincinnati Ballet's new web site: home page with rotating main image, above; dancers' bio page, far right; and the "inside the ballet" page, right.

The Web Site

Botts describes the digital design process: "We incorporated key design elements from our graphic designers and maintained the elegance and movement developed on the print solutions. Using these key elements, we were able to make the technology appear transparent, removing the gap between print and web."

"We apply web standards to our viewable page size and to the page file size. We utilized Flash to maintain a sense of movement without large file downloads. The challenge is to deliver the page quickly without sacrificing the brand identity, and we accomplished that on the Cincinnati Ballet web site."

147A

identity

VMA's move to the "Firefly Building" in 2001 created the opportunity to completely rethink their identity. The partners wanted to create an environment to both attract and retain the type of talent they were after. They also wanted to use the space as a marketing tool for their clients—to have a comfortable space they were all proud to share. Their new print and web materials reflect this pride.

57B

Paper is an important element of the stationery. The mix of translucent, opaque and colored papers adds variety and freshness.

148A

The VMA web site reflects their creativity. Its Flash animation and changing imagery are dynamic and energetic. The use of translucency and color directly connect with the other identity materials.

In this promotional piece, individual pages can be reordered and exchanged to focus and update information.

"Design-driven branding:
The most powerful brands are experiences,
the culmination of all of the
design elements that define them.
At VMA, we maximize the design
and ultimately the experience."
– www.vmai.com

The Approach: Develop strong relationships so you can work with people you like.

SamataMason
MVP.com

Locations:

West Dundee, IL

Vancouver, BC

Principals:

Dave Mason

Pat Samata

Greg Samata

Staff:

Chicago: 15

Vancouver: 2

 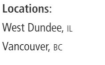

The Firm

In 1995, Samata Associates and Dave Mason & Associates joined to form SamataMason, a multifaceted design firm working across media, including print, digital, environmental, signage and film/video. Lead by three principals with forty-five years of combined design 54B ⊙ experience, the firm expertly handles all aspects of corporate communications, identity, marketing and image management from their converted bowling alley office in West Dundee, Illinois and their harborfront loft in Vancouver, British Columbia.

Dave Mason describes the firm's move to a holistic approach: "Greg and I were both known for annual report design. Technology has driven us to a point where we can expand our disciplines and affect other mediums. Our clients count on us to be smart enough to extend their message across all media. We do television commercials, radio commercials, ads, annual reports, packaging, print. There isn't much we can't do, and I believe this is the future of the design business. We have the desire to do it. We have an interest in wanting to do everything. We are sixteen people that act like a hundred. We name companies. We do research. We do big companies."

"Companies want to work with people they like—the relationship is increasingly important to them. They want to have a comfort level with you and if they do, they will give you the work," concludes Mason.

The Client Project

MVP.com is a great example of SamataMason's philosophy, "We do good work for good people. And have fun doing it." According to their annual report, "MVP.com, acquired by CBS SportsLine.com, was the premier source for sports, fitness and outdoor equipment and apparel on the Internet. The site featured equipment and advice from the MVP.com advisory board, made up of some of the world's top athletes, such as John Elway, Michael Jordan and Wayne Gretzky."

The services provided to MVP.com included advertising, collateral, copywriting, film/video, identity and web design. Greg Samata describes the logo development: "The obvious direction for us was to do a macho MVP sports jersey look, but the demographics were skewed to women. Not that men weren't buying, but more women were buying online products at the time. We realized that if we tried to create a brand that was gender specific that would be a mistake. MVP.com had to be neutral. It also had to be a 'non-brand' so it didn't compete with all the other highly visual sports logos and icons that it had to coexist with."

The web site and the business were driven by championship testimonials and expertise and knowledge in every area of sports. The site was more than a place to buy equipment. It was a place to get detailed technical specifications, product quality information and advice from champions. This educational component differentiated the site from the competition.

MVP.com logo.

75B

151A

HelveticaNeue Black Extended
ABCDEFGHIJKLMNOPQRSTUVWXYZ
abcdefghijklmnopqrstuvwxyz
1234567890

HelveticaNeue Extended
ABCDEFGHIJKLMNOPQRSTUVWXYZ
abcdefghijklmnopqrstuvwxyz
1234567890

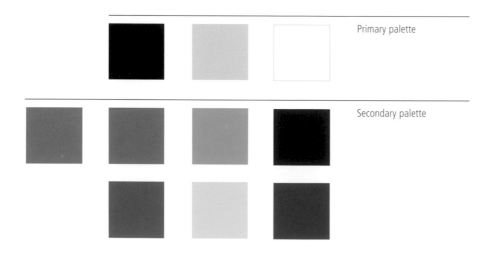

Primary palette

Secondary palette

The Brand Rules and Tools

HelveticaNeue Extended and HelveticaNeue Black Extended were the typefaces used in the logo and throughout the applications. This type family accomplished the goal of design "neutrality." The extended characters also work well with the form of most sports logotypes, and they gave a bold, contemporary feel to the mark.

The primary color palette was also clean and neutral, living well with the wide variety of sports team and product palettes. The secondary palette, which was used on the web site for color-coding the various sections, played up on the colors associated with various sports: orange for basketball, blue for ice hockey and brown for football, for example.

Photographic imagery bought texture and energy to the brand identity. Tightly cropped shots of sports equipment, shown right, provided an innovative and highly graphic look to familiar objects.

These tightly cropped images of sports equipment were used in such applications as business cards and the web site.

153A

MVP.com limited-edition poster.

The Process

Greg Samata talks about the firm's process: "We listen. We ask a lot of dumb questions. We're not experts at what our customers do for a living, they are. We ask the questions that an internal person would feel foolish asking. From those answers we derive key points. It's about message content—and if we get the message right, the design presents itself, so we work really hard at finding out what the message is. That's the process. The design part is actually easy. Design is the fun part."

Samata continues, "From MVP, we learned so much about relationships, not just technology. About what people think and about what they buy on the web. About how people relate to you as a business when they don't meet you."

He explains their attitude toward consumer research: "We tested the site to some extent. But we've found that your intuition and your gut instincts are more important today then ever. You may have $250,000 to do focus group testing, but do you need it? Isn't there enough knowledge in history and the marketplace to direct your decisions?"

20B-23B

69B

MVP.com corporate brochure.

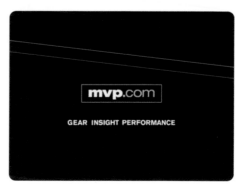

MVP.com launch video sample screens.

The Applications

There were a number of print and video applications that supported the web site and the business in general. Samata describes the work: "There was obviously a carry-through in attitude and physical look among the pieces. The differences were that the web site was supposed to be a functional operating mechanism, where the other things are static objects, whether they are business cards or brochures." The video components, as well as the launch video and instructional videos, added excitement, energy, movement and sound to the identity.

155A

The Michael Jordan instructional video sample screens, part of the educational component of the web site, mixed more straightforward video of Jordan with exciting and energetic graphics and typography.

The Web Site

So what made this site special? It was the first time in history that anybody was trying to sell every conceivable kind of sports equipment online. Plus, you could get advice on what equipment to buy and how to shoot a free throw from Michael Jordan. Plus, you could get demonstration videos to download, shown left. At the turn of the twenty-first century, this was very comprehensive and revolutionary for the web.

75B

"Not only did the design have to be good, and the architecture had to work, but we had to try to find new ways of merchandising these products and new ways of advertising products online," explains Samata.

PROCESS TIP

SamataMason develops strategic relationships with writers and researchers to extend their capabilities and give them flexibility in picking just the right people for the specific client job.

"At the same time we codeveloped a web site feedback system called Online Opinion. It allowed users to give quantitative and qualitative feedback about the way the site worked and looked. This made the web experience a truly interactive media for the user instead of just having them stare at the screen like a television. "In the first week after the site launched, users gave them feedback about what was missing. Some were simple things and some were more in-depth. "It was very helpful to MVP in terms of managing their business based on absolutely direct comments from their actual customers," concludes Samata.

MVP.com retail web site sample pages for basketball, rugby, ice hockey and baseball. Color-coding of the various sections clarified and simplified the site for users.

identity

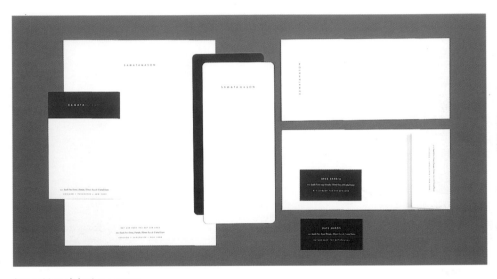

SamataMason's business papers.

Clear and compelling communication is at the heart of SamataMason's own identity, as well as the work they do for their clients. Dave Mason elaborates, "Our clients build their own brands. We help them articulate their messages and communicate in a way that is unique, meaningful, compelling and consistent. We help put a 'face' on something intangible and, if we do our part right, we contribute to our clients' success."

"We're lucky. For the most part we work with people who feel the same way about their companies and their brands as we do about our own. They're proud of what they do and what they stand for, and they care about communicating well. And when it's all real there's nothing more powerful."

S A M A T A M A S O N

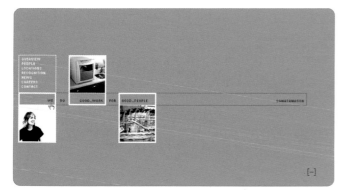

SamataMason's web site is organized around their mission statement, "We do good work for good people." Shown are the home page, above, a portfolio page, top right, and a client page, bottom right.

Each year SamataMason creates an annual report highlighting their projects from the previous year.

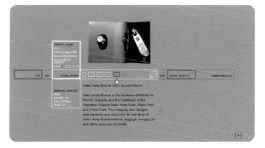

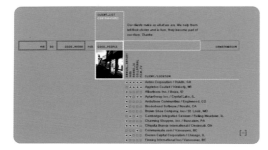

Colophon

Design Alliance was produced in QuarkXPress, with the assistance of Adobe Photoshop, Adobe Illustrator, Macromedia FreeHand, and Microsoft Word on my beloved PowerBook G4, "Mr. Peabody." Assistance was rendered by my desktop G4, "Mr. Wizard."

Frutiger, designed by Adrienne Frutiger in 1975, is the main type family used throughout the body and cover of the book. It was chosen for its wonderful balance between the technical/geometric, (symbolizing interactive media) and the organic/humanistic, (symbolizing traditional media). The additional typefaces and families are identified in each chapter.

More advice, ideas and inspiration from HOW Design Books!

Inspiration is key to your success as a designer. It makes you more creative, energetic and competitive. Unfortunately, inspiration doesn't always come when and where you want it. *Idea Revolution* includes 120 activities, exercises and anecdotes that will jolt you, your colleagues and your clients back to creative life. You'll find unique, motivational solutions to virtually every graphic challenge.

ISBN 1-58180-332-X, paperback, 160 pages, #32300-K

Graphically Speaking breaks down designer-client dialogue into something both parties can understand. It details 31 buzzwords (such as "innovative" or "kinetic") related to the most-requested design styles. Each entry is defined both literally and graphically with designer commentary and visual reference materials, ensuring clear designer-client communication every time!

ISBN 1-58180-291-9, hardcover, 240 pages, #32168-K

Turn an impossible deadline into a realistic schedule. Identify problem areas before you start working. Master software and production techniques that save time and money. Produce good design on even the tightest budget. Pat Matson Knapp shows you how to do all this and more to beat project constraints and create head-turning designs every time.

ISBN 1-58180-331-1, hardcover, 192 pages, #32297-K

These books and other fine HOW Design titles are available from your local bookstore or online supplier, or by calling 1-800-448-0915.

08 07 06 05 04   1 2 3 4 5

Library of Congress Cataloging-in-Publication Data

Faimon, Peg, 1962–
    Design alliance : uniting print + Web design to create a total brand presence / Peg Faimon.
        p. cm.
    Includes bibliographical references and index.
    ISBN 1-58180-400-8 (hc w/wire)
    1. Web sites--Design--Case Studies. 2. Website development industry. 3. Internet marketing. 4. Commercial art. 5. Brand name products. 6. Web site development--Glossaries. I. Title.

TK5105.888.F353 2003
005.7'2--dc21

2003049965

Editor: Amy Schell
Cover and Interior Design: Peg Faimon
In-house Creative Consultant: Lisa Buchanan
Production Coordinator: Sara Dumford
Photographer, unless otherwise noted: Christine Polomsky

The permissions on pages 150B–151B constitute an extension of this copyright page.

CONTEXT & REFERENCE

How to Use This Book

Consistent, evolving and flexible application of brand identity is needed to clearly communicate the brand's core values in this competitive, fast-paced and international market. Does today's access to both print and digital media provide a better way to integrate all of the brand's elements and applications into a strategic design package to meet clients' needs? Of course! This book demonstrates how, through the blending of traditional and interactive media, designers can strengthen not only the recognition of their clients' brands but also their clients' customer communications and, ultimately, their own business.

So why is this book organized and structured the way it is? What are those icons doing in the page gutters? And what are the numbers under them? The structure of the book reflects the nonlinear organization of the web. The icons in the gutters on the top pages show you what section to reference on the bottom pages, and the number indicates the specific page.

So, for instance, say you come across a specific design firm's particular process in the text, and you want to find out more about the process of branding in general. Look for the icon and page number in the gutter and, without losing your place, turn the pages of the bottom section until you come to additional resources in the section called Alliance + Process: Print and Web. In this way, you can access two different pieces of information at the same time, similar to searching on the web.

Along the same lines, if you come across a word you are not familiar with, or simply want to know a little more about a particular concept, there are two full glossaries of terms in the bottom matter. The first one contains terms from the world of online design and marketing, while the second contains terms specific to branding.

So, this unusual structure is not only a gimmick to make the book look cool. It is a functional concept created to be helpful and useful to you, the reader. It should make your reading and learning more efficient and enjoyable.

**Quotes From Professionals:
The Branding Landscape**

Branding is a term with which we are all familiar—both design professionals and the general public. Over the last decade, "brand" and "branding" have become household words, and their true meaning has become confused. During the interviews with design and business professionals that resulted in the case studies above, one of the key questions for the fifteen strategic design firms was, "How does your firm define branding?" Their answers convey the philosophy of the designers and their clients and clarify the meaning and importance of the branding process. You may notice a common thread among the responses, but also note the interesting nuances and individuality of each response as well.

"Branding is everything that makes up a company—the face of a company."
Nina Dietzel, 300FeetOut

"A brand is a company's most important asset. You are going to live or die by how your brand is recognized. A strong brand is one that can deliver on a promise."
David Warren, Tank Design

"A brand identity is a visual, verbal, and conceptual kit of parts that communicates a coherent and unified message in a multitude of ways to a multitude of audiences."
P. Michael Zender, Zender + Associates

"Companies need to align their employees with the brand promise so they live the brand."
Garry Naifeh, Monigle Associates

"Branding is certainly more than a logo. Branding is a promise to deliver the best possible products or services to a loyal customer base. A brand is really a commitment to standards that are upheld and consistently reinforced."
Ken Carbone, Carbone Smolan Agency

11B

"Is it a logo? A color? A tagline? Or something more? There is one answer to all these questions: A brand is everything. Everything from how we answer the phone to the reliability of our products and services. A company's brand is its most valuable asset. Brands are what our customers identify with when they choose to do business with us. More than that, our brand represents a promise to our consumers that it must live up to. Creating and maintaining a viable brand is a time-honored process of construction, adjustment and ongoing effort."
Inforonics Brand Manual

"A brand is something a group of individuals has to be committed to. It's like raising a child."
Scott Watts, Tank Design

"Developing a strong brand involves questioning all aspects of a company's behavior."
Robbie Laughton, Wolff Olins

"Branding is the essence of a company, a product, or place. Good ones deliver consistent messages, images, voice and personality. They must be very carefully thought through."
Kiku Obata, Kiku Obata

"The brand is the heart and soul of a given company—the personality of the company. Brand is really taking the core essence and trying to distill it so that it is clear, understandable, and compelling to a given audience set."
Steven Morris, Morris Creative

"Branding is incredibly holistic and it's for the life of the company."
Fred Weaver, Tank Design

"Branding takes in all of the traditional design principles and elements—the type of photography, color, illustration, typography, texture and then having all of those applied to different components—print, digital, etc. Have a consistent message throughout all of those pieces."
Kenneth Botts, Visual Marketing Associates

13B

"It's a term that has become so popular, growing out of traditional graphic design and corporate identity—stuff graphic designers have been practicing for years. It's the consistency, the voice, the positioning—any contact you have with the consumer."
Rich Rico, The VIA Group

"Branding should target the head and heart."
Jamie Koval, VSA Partners

"Branding is a multidimensional approach to communicating an idea or essence that connects to its audiences on both the emotional and rational levels. A brand must be authentic, delivering on its promises and staying true to its purposes. The first step is developing a partnership with your client. You have to develop a brand's vocabulary and consistently look ahead for ways to achieve goals beyond what the client might be thinking."
Mike Weikert, Iconologic

"Branding is both the science and the art of making products, services and ideas distinguishable from one another."
Juliet D'Ambrosio, Iconologic

"Over the last couple of years, branding has become an important internal tool. It has become as valuable for companies to rally around their own brand as a way of motivating, as a way of bringing a sense of unity and vision that may have been overlooked before. It's interesting the buzz that happens as that manifests itself both from an external, and internal, view."
Sue Nixon, Leonhardt:Fitch

"What we try to do is find what the brand is and paint a picture of it so people can understand it. We deliver the brand in a visual sense and an attitudinal sense, into meanings that work for the client, but ultimately we can't create the brand. That's up to the company and its employees."
Greg Samata, SamataMason

15B

"Brand is a promise or an unwritten contract between the company/product and the consumer. A strong brand has a clear, relevant and sustainable point of differentiation relative to the competition. The brand must stand for something. It must have a place in the consumer's mind.

Often, people confuse branding with advertising. A brand strategically defines the core attributes and personality of the product, service or company. These unique attributes are then communicated visually through design—typically as packaging or a corporate identity. Advertising should take its cues from brand strategy, embodying and reflecting the personality of the brand. In addition, advertising campaigns are designed to run for months at a time, while branding is longer term, more strategic in nature and influenced less by trends."

Hayes Roth, Landor

In the course of speaking with all these talented and intelligent individuals, and doing all the traditional research that such a book requires, I came to realize that one of the most important characteristics of branding—and design for that matter—is its evolutionary nature. The development of a brand is what brings it to life for those charged with its growth and for those observing and interacting with it. Additionally, brands are fragile. They require thoughtful, dedicated and responsible individuals for creation, administration and implementation.

Alliance and Process: Print + Web

Changing Times

They say times have changed. But is it true? As a culture, what reflects that change? What tells us that we need to redefine our paradigms, that we need to rethink how we do business and communicate with our employees and consumers? Technological developments over the last decade have transformed our society and the way we do business. With the development of interactive media we have the opportunity to communicate in new and faster ways. But does that mean the old ways are outdated? Have they been completely replaced with these new communications tools?

As a graphic design professional and educator, I say "no." Print media (brochures, periodicals, annual reports, promotional materials, packaging, etc.) and interactive media (web sites, interactive CDs, Flash animations, etc.) can and should coexist in alliance with one another. I would submit that the best way to communicate with customers today is an integrative approach using both the traditional and the new. Print and interactive media communicate in different ways and with different audiences; there is a time and place for both in the integrated branding experience.

This isn't always what happens in the professional world, nor is it what students are taught in academia. Our culture tends toward compartmentalization. Integration and connections are not easy to achieve, and people generally aren't taught to solve problems from a global perspective. Seeing the big picture is becoming more and more important in our increasingly complex world; therefore, we need to take a new approach to our work and to educating future professionals.

Technology is becoming so familiar that it will soon be invisible to us—an expectation.

The innovations of interactive media will continue but we will no longer be infatuated with this new toy in the same way as in the last decade.

Sue Nixon, CEO of Leonhardt:Fitch in Seattle, speaks to this point: "Technology will never replace good thinking. Ultimately, the designer must come up with innovative solutions no matter what the landscape. No longer is it cool to have technology; it's required. Designers need to be more versatile because you never know what media will be needed. And media inter-relate—if a logo design can't translate into web, you're suddenly isolating a huge audience. All the factors must be considered."

Brand Process

With all these changes and the evolution in media, one thing has remained essentially unchanged— the core design process. In the case studies above, each firm discusses their process as a general approach, highlighting the specific details for the project discussed. Each has their own unique twist, whether it is a specific problem-solving approach or a name with which they have branded their individual process. But when compared one to another, they have many similarities. Generally speaking, across media, it is a logical progression:

1 Information gathering and analysis of the client and the brand's positive attributes

2 Research, determination and analysis of the target audience(s)

3 Development of the brand architecture and brand essence (a brief phrase that describes the brand), positioning (benefits and points of difference from the competition) and strategy

4   Creative development in all appropriate media

5   Refinement and measurement

6   Implementation and production

7   Development of a plan for future growth and
evolution of the brand

For a start-up company, obviously there is a blank slate on which to create. Although the client may have ideas and notions about what they are looking for, the consumer has no predetermined notions or perceptions about the company. For an existing company it works a bit differently. For a brand revitalization, the designer needs to assess what's currently working for the brand so that the baby's not thrown out with the bath water. Certain brand equities may be retained, giving some continuity to the change.

Ultimately, changes and additions to the brand—its evolution—are essential to giving it life and keeping it up-to-date. It's important to plan for such changes so the brand does not become stagnant and lose its relevance to the target audience.

An Example of Brand Structure & Integration

Monigle Associates, Denver, Colorado, has developed an effective graphic, referred to as the "brandscape," for clearly representing the relationship of brand elements (see far right). For Monigle, as for most companies, brand essence resides at the core of the brand. Reflecting out from the essence are the core identity elements: the name, design and brand structure. Beyond these are communications elements: advertising, print collateral, product ID, signage, web sites, uniforms, environments, packaging, etc. Interactive, print and environmental design are thoroughly integrated and appropriately chosen for execution given the project and problem solution. In the outer ring, supporting the inside elements, are the actions, performance, service and quality of the company, employees and product—delivering on the brand promise.

Monigle's "Top 10 Key Benefits of a Strong Brand" include the following:

1 Differentiation/Positioning

2 Communication of an Accurate, Clear and Consistent Image

3 Consumer Awareness and Loyalty

4 Provides a Shortcut For Consumer Decision-making

5 Provides a "Halo" of Credibility For Subsidiaries, Products, Services and Extensions

6 Price Premium

7 Internal Unity and Focus

8 Strong Defense Against Negatives and Competitive Encroachments

9 Cost Efficiencies In Communication and Purchasing

10 Market Clout

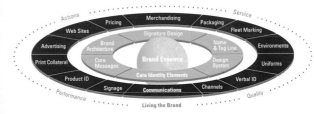

Branding's Past: A Brief Look

Brand is an English word, derived from "torch." It refers to the burning of a mark of an owner or maker onto wooden and metal products, domestic animals, and other goods and property.

The phenomenon of branding goes back some five thousand years to the beginnings of economic history. There is evidence that brands were used in ancient Egypt on domesticated animals to mark ownership. Printers' marks, from the fifteenth century, identified the quality of printing execution. And silversmiths over the centuries, including Paul Revere, pressed marks into their products indicating the quality of the metal and the craftsmanship. These forerunners to modern trademarks and brands desired social identification and proof of ownership and product origin.

Historically, there was a transition from the brand identifying an individual to the brand representing a larger organization or company. This change in the perception of brands was key to building the contemporary power of branding.

"Josiah Wedgwood is often cited as the father of the modern brand. Beginning in the 1760s, Wedgwood placed his name on his pottery and china to indicate their source — his-state-of-the-art factories — and therefore their quality. But the Wedgwood name came to stand for something more. Nearly two hundred years before the advent of mass media, and without using conventional advertising, Wedgwood used royal endorsements and other marketing devices to create an aura around the name of his company that gave the brand a value far beyond the attributes of the product itself." (www.lippincottmercer.com, "Rethinking Brand Strategy: A 'Mindshare' Manifesto," Eric Almquist and Kenneth J. Roberts)

The move to a mass-market economy occurred with the end of World War II, resulting from an increase in consumption, the baby boom and the development of television. Advertising agencies responded to this situation by creating mass campaigns, primarily for consumer products. Today we see this phenomenon in the Super Bowl, which draws an enormous audience to not only watch football but also experience the debut of the latest and greatest in television advertising campaigns.

In the past, the advertising agency model has dominated brand management. In fact, many business executives still think of working with ad agencies when they wish to build their brands. But with the evolution of the marketplace, this model is rapidly becoming obsolete. The mass market has become more diversified to meet more specific customer needs. It is being replaced by a wide array of communications channels and media that are capable of targeting increasingly narrow customer segments. Much of this new capability is due to developments in technology. Longevity and endurance are no longer enough to make a successful brand. In today's volatile business environment, brands need to be flexible, evolving and responsive—or they will quickly become irrelevant.

In "A 'Mindshare' Manifesto," by Eric Almquist and Kenneth J. Roberts, five current branding misconceptions are addressed. Many of these ideas have grown out of the history of branding. As we move into the 21st century, Almquist and Roberts note that businesses need to rethink the branding process to avoid these common misconceptions:

1 "Brands are built mainly through advertising."

With the customer experience often paramount, many of today's great brands are built with little to no advertising.

2 "Brands are used to influence customers."

While this is true, it is also very important to influence current and prospective employees and investors.

3 "The key to successful brand management involves understanding the effectiveness of the brand in today's marketplace."

This is important, but being able to anticipate a brand's relevance to the most valuable customers of tomorrow is crucial. The brand must be flexible and forward thinking.

4 "Brands are symbolic and emotive and therefore are managed primarily through 'creativity' rather than analysis."

There must be a balance between the heart and the head. Brands can be analyzed with economic rigor.

5 "Brands are the responsibility of the marketing department."

Brands are everyone's responsibility. Employee buy-in across departments and levels of hierarchy is extremely important so the brand promise is delivered with consistency and enthusiasm.

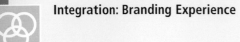
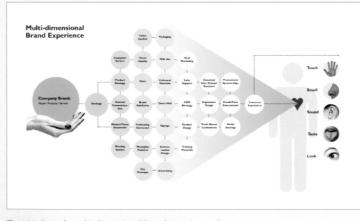

The VIA Group's multi-dimensional brand experience chart

is just part of the branding package. "Ultimately, a well-designed identity is a reflection of the business it symbolizes. It is a gesture of goodwill and sends the message that the company or organization cares about its audience," according to the VIA Group's multi-dimensional brand experience chart. In the past, designers were asked to develop corporate identity solely in the form of logos and their applications, like stationery, packaging, promotional pieces, and signage. But that's changed.

Corporate Identity to Branding: Designer to Strategic Design Partner

The Evolution of "Design"

There are many reasons for the evolution from corporate identity to branding:

1 Today's consumers and companies are more sophisticated. "The general public is becoming smarter, more educated, more aware of design and the quality of design."
("Corporate and Brand Identity: New Challenges, New Competition," *Graphic Design USA*, April 2002: p.59)

2 Consumers face a growing number of choices in every category of product and service. How are they to differentiate between them?

3 Consumers are looking to develop relationships with companies and brands. What they drive, eat and play with is important to them

and possibly identifies them. There is a new need to convey approachability—to connect on an emotional level.

4 Following the dot.com era, and the dishonesty of companies like Enron and WorldCom, consumers are skeptical, and rightly so. Do they trust the brands they have come to know and love? It has become very important to actually BE honest and authentic to consumers and not just look it on a superficial level. According to Ken Carbone, of the Carbone Smolan Agency, "It's a company saying, 'We're a great company, we're going to stay that way. We're really going to pay attention to who we are as a brand.' That kind of commitment is very magnetic. People start to recognize that consistent commitment to quality standards. It's what builds brand loyalty and ultimately results in the growth of profitability."

This is as important internally as externally. If your own employees don't believe in you, who will? "Companies need to align their employees with the brand promise so they live the brand," says Garry Naifeh, Monigle Associates. This approach has resulted in a new trend to educate employees more fully about the brand, helping them communicate its goals and messages more accurately and consistently to external audiences. It's vitally important that all employees buy into the brand and understand how to articulate its message so this consistency is maintained. Every time an employee opens their mouth to speak with a customer, they are communicating the brand—and it can just as easily be a positive or a negative interaction.

Having a nice logo and visually unified stationery and signage simply isn't enough anymore. All of a company's messages must be consistent across media—from the web site to direct mail to a retail environment to the way the salesperson answers the phone to the music that's played when the consumer is on hold.

Many times this requires a culture change within a company. "Developing a brand involves questioning all aspects of a company's behavior," says Robbie Laughton, from Wolff Olins. This sometimes requires a complete overhaul of long-held beliefs and patterns of corporate behavior.

For example, in their work with Axeda, not only did The VIA Group help them with positioning, identity development and branding, but they are helping them gear up for a comprehensive roll-out. They have created the advertising, the direct mail and the web site. "All of the various customer touch points and interactions with the brand will be developed by us. So when this thing rolls out, it will be very cohesive," says Rich Rico. This is what builds consumer confidence and trust.

This change has also required design firms to rethink their approaches. Firms must now keep up with new communications options and tools, such as opt-in e-mail and web sitelets. Rico continues, "'Although we are true believers in the printed medium and papers, you can also leverage electronic media…but it's got to be part of an overall mix. You can't depend upon any one medium.'" ("Corporate and Brand Identity: New Challenges, New Competition," *Graphic Design USA*, April 2002: p.59)

The Evolution of "Designer"

Tom Webb of Monigle Associates says, "Designers are being forced to be business thinkers, not only knowing the language of business but understanding what moves businesses. What drives growth. What motivates customers in a particular industry. The idea of a designer as a decorator is a dinosaur."

Designers are thinking more strategically and are more business-focused. Many firms have the foundation phase and a creative strategy phase—interviews, research and analysis of the client and their customers from which a creative strategy is developed, which may include a name change, positioning or a creative plan.

Designers are adapting to this evolution, realizing that strong brands are created through strategic thinking, specifically:

1 Being selective and thoughtful in developing their targets

2 Searching for unique consumer insights through careful research

3 Making and keeping a distinctive promise to the consumer

4 Developing a unique and differentiating image consistent to the promise

5 Organizing and structuring a brand architecture that makes sense in the marketplace

6 Changing and influencing consumer and employee behavior

7 Balancing the evolution of the brand with a need for consistency and familiarity

As Mike Zender, Founder of Zender + Associates points out, "Over ten years ago, it was common for us to be handed a brief or project description. We'd certainly be handed the content, and that is the exception now instead of the rule. We are involved with coming up with what should be said, who it should be said to, how it should be said and then designing what should be said. That is a really big change. That's where we wanted to be many years ago, but nobody would take us seriously. The Internet—and technology—really helped open the door for this new approach." Much of the bread-and-butter production work was taken in-house during the 1980s, resulting in design firms needing to go lower and take in more production work or go in the opposite direction and move up the economic and professional ladder into a more strategic, business focused position.

This is an exciting time for designers. This evolution brings with it greater responsibility and challenge, things most designers thrive on. It has redefined our industry and our client relationships.

Print vs. Web: Friends or Foes?

Not so long ago, when the web and interactive media first came into popular use, people predicted the end of print communications. Books and brochures would no longer be needed because we'd have everything readily accessible on the web. With just a click and a scroll we could get any and all information we'd ever want. But, as you know, that hasn't come to pass.

As the initial wonder of the Internet wears off, we have discovered the appeal of the printed piece is still strong, and the need for paper is even growing. Print and web are different; they're both good at some things and not so good at other things. Sue Nixon of Leonhardt:Fitch says, "It's like currency. Debit cards, credit cards and checks have not made cash and coins obsolete. They are merely additional choices in the consumer's palette. Print and web are merely options in the communications palette."

Traditional Media

The tangible and tactile quality of print communications brings authenticity and permanence to a message. From an early age we learn to trust what is in print and believe it to be true. An e-mail is sufficient for casual correspondence, but when you want to provide formal or very important information, you send a letter. Paper tends to be symbolic of quality and importance. If a message is more enduring, a printed piece gives a personal touch.

An annual report, for instance, with all of its financial information, is more believable in print. Also, the density of the information, in text and chart form, is often more clearly communicated, and at a higher resolution. Donna Torrance, Strategic Principal for The VIA Group's New York studio, cautions about web-based annual reports: "While the web versions of annual reports are almost becoming de rigueur, these online spin-offs are unlikely to overtake traditional ink-on-paper

annuals. Information gleaned from the web is immediately available, but too often it lacks the vision and magic that print media accompanied by compelling photographs, graphs or illustrations can provide. Balance is necessary, and the dynamic, immediate experience of the online annual report must complement and be consistent with the permanence and credibility inherent in a printed annual report."

Interactive Media

The web, on the other hand, is great for quickly changing and widely distributing information. "What technology does very well is open doors, start conversations, pique interest" (Aaron Kwittken, "Is Paper the Most Advanced Communications Media?," www.vianow.com). It is obviously superior to paper in providing and storing large amounts of data quickly. The potential for animation and sound and the power of motion graphics can bring excitement and energy to a message. Also, the nonlinear nature of interactive media means the viewer perceives that they have "more control" of the content, and their choices are increased.

A combination of user control over the web experience and the inherent lack of detailed design control can sometimes compromise the consistency of the brand's visual message. For example, the design of the page and the content can shift and distort from browser to browser, and the user can change their font choice and size. These may seem like small problems to the non-designer, but when trying to maintain consistency in look and feel across media, the lack of control over these details can be frustrating. What has resulted is a more flexible approach for the web in

many cases. The main brand elements are generally maintained, with more variety at a certain level of design detail.

Nina Dietzel of 300FeetOut says, "I think it has impacted aesthetics in a certain way. It always has to be good design, but you have to simplify things for the web. You cannot work in as many layers of information. Things that might look great in print, and things that you might interact with for a longer period of time in print, just don't work on the web. So you have to be very straightforward, very direct, to empower the user and let them interact with your site."

Design Alliance

Opposites attract. The careful coordination of traditional and new media means covering all the bases of communications. For some types of products or services, one may dominate due to target audience needs, but in most cases a combination of the two results in the most effective delivery of the message. The integration of the two is also increasingly important, because audience behavior increasingly demands multiple channels of interaction and connection.

For example, Mike Zender, of Zender + Associates in Cincinnati, Ohio, explains, "I can't really conceive of us doing an identity for someone that doesn't have a time-based version. For some clients the time-based version is more significant and more interesting than the static one." This means that the functional and aesthetic requirements for identities have changed. Logos not only have to work at various sizes and color applications but at various speeds.

It is very important for designers to not only understand how to coordinate print and web but also when to choose each medium. In what circumstance should you choose print, and when should you choose to communicate through the web or interactive media? In making this decision, consider the audience and what they are looking for—whether it is facts and clear informational content or more of a user experience where they can feel like a part of the action. Also consider the complexity or simplicity of the message to be communicated, the type of information or data, and the requirements for the quality level of imagery. As Stephen Greco comments, "The most exciting potential…is the coexistence of print and the web. The web is about how it works, not how it looks," he says. "If you try to articulate the virtues of beautiful design as you can on paper, it will be fake. What you want is louder… faster…funnier…the next screen in a fraction of a second. You want navigational strategies that get you there without making you stop and think about context—unlike a paper volume, in which you turn the page and know where you are with respect to the whole. The web is superbly adapted to daily news, but not to the contents of an art book" (www.vianow.com, "Is Paper the Most Advanced Communications Medium?").

**Interdisciplinary Approach:
Design Profession and Education**

A Holistic, Team-based Approach

In the early days of the web, many companies commissioned their print design and advertising through one or even two firms and their web site through a separate firm specializing in interactive design. These "boutiques" still produce a fair quantity of work. Recently, in an effort to be more holistic and cost effective, many companies have simplified matters and are taking their design needs to more comprehensive and integrated firms capable of doing, or at least closely managing, all media. This more holistic approach can result in a very cohesive design strategy and implementation. Strategic brand identity programs often consist of renaming, a brand manual, a new logo, rollout materials, brand voice, giveaway items, advertising, signage, banners, business papers, brochures, publications, packaging and a web site.

These types of projects require a broad range of skills. This means teamwork—print, environmental and package designers; marketing and business specialists; creative writers and technical communicators; public relations specialists; interactive and web designers; programmers, etc. The individual discipline doesn't seem to be as important as the approach to problem solving and creative thinking. Innovation is key. The ability to understand and work in multidisciplinary teams is essential. "You need wildly creative people that love to challenge every assumption. You need very careful and detail-oriented people. You need very creative, problem-solving, analytical people to come up with the strategies. You need wise people who have real insight based on knowledge put into appropriate context."

(Mike Zender, Zender + Associates)

55B

Growth in the Competitive Set

As was noted in the April 2002 article in *Graphic Design USA*, "Corporate and Brand Identity: New Challenges, New Competition," traditional design firms are beginning to feel the pressure from a broader competitive set. Management and business consultants are seeing the value of offering the more tactical side of brand identity development—how do you really connect with your audience in a tangible way? Even firms traditionally known for product design, such as frog design, are moving into the world of branding. In the article, Gregory Horn notes that "'frog was known first and foremost as an industrial design firm....We were developing our clients' brands through product design, and we had an intimate knowledge of that area...so who better to help them develop things like a sub-brand logo, packaging, collateral?

It was a natural evolution for our group to grow that way,' he said."

Within this competitive environment it makes sense for firms to broaden their capabilities and offerings, either in-house or with interdisciplinary partnerships. Clients need the marketing and business knowledge, two- and three-dimensional experience, and interactive expertise in today's marketplace. This "one-stop shopping" means more convenience for the client and more control for the designer. It may also mean a deeper, richer business relationship that will result in a more quality solution.

Developing Young Designers

In this changing culture, design and creative directors must take the lead to ensure an innovative and stimulating environment for their young design employees. VSA Partners pride themselves on having such an environment. As a visitor, when I entered their open and brightly lit office, the space seemed full of energy. Process work was openly displayed throughout the studio. There were gatherings of employees in two meeting rooms on either side of the entrance. Through the glass walls and doors I could see what appeared to be a critique going on. Everyone was freely sharing their ideas and there didn't seem to be an apparent hierarchy among the participants. As Jamie Koval remarks, "It's a very informal environment. To me it feels more like a university. We do a lot of critiques."

At Leonhardt:Fitch in Seattle, CEO Sue Nixon also understands the importance of developing young talent. "The creative lead works very hard at creating a safe place to critique so that early on, entering the firm, young creatives get comfortable with putting their work on the wall and explaining why they did what they did and what client objective they are trying to articulate with their specific direction. This elevates the design to a new level, and refinements are based on the feedback that they get within the session. It also helps our designers to be very articulate about what they are doing, so when it comes to creative presentations to clients, it's always the designers that are presenting their own work."

Back at School

Most professionals discover the importance of integration, connection and context in the workplace, because many educational settings simply don't provide an interdisciplinary or integrated curriculum where students of different majors work together to solve multidimensional problems. Why do we expect them to successfully jump to this type of problem-solving behavior immediately upon graduation?

Communication is becoming more complex. It's harder, if not impossible, for an individual to solve such problems. It requires a team-based approach. Within the team, specialized knowledge is still important, perhaps even more so than in the past. As before, students need to learn enough about their own discipline to perform their tasks and solve their assigned problems with innovation and efficiency. The new twist is that they no longer work in isolation. Additional skills are required, including the ability to clearly and effectively communicate with others on the team. Also, every discipline has its own language, and students need, at the very least, to have a basic understanding of the vocabulary of the other disciplines they will most likely be working with.

Here are some suggestions for curriculum enhancements:

1. Build upon existing discipline-specific (specialist) courses to develop multidisciplinary, team-based capstone courses that focus on multidimensional complex problem-solving.

2. Develop a more integrated, less compartmentalized curriculum. Make any and all attempts to point out connections within and between courses and skill sets.

3. Develop a strong communication network between departments and disciplines. Encourage faculty and students to work with those outside their discipline.

4. Develop courses that teach organizational, project management, and communications skills through real-world project-based experiences.

5 Develop courses that focus on the psychology of teamwork.

6 Challenge students to think creatively. Encourage innovation and independent thinking!

During the interviews with the designers featured in the case studies above, many people noted that the definition of "designer" will change in the future. A common thread in the responses was one of designer as director/producer. The skill set for designers is continually growing, and ultimately we will be required to do so many different things that it will be impossible to be an expert at any one thing. Perhaps that day has already come? The best designers may become more like director/pro-ducers—putting together a team of people and working in concert with them to produce the best possible product—a project manager, so to speak. Even if this doesn't come to pass, it is fair to say that collaboration will play a much greater role in the future definition of "designer."

Following are thoughts from design and business professionals about current and future trends in branding, technology and design. What's in store for the future?

Branding

1 Brand Differentiation

Many established companies are reevaluating their brands and thinking about their perception in the marketplace. How do their audiences interact with their various brands? How can they connect more directly to their consumers? Customers have a staggering number of choices, and those choices are growing each year. The effective communication of differentiating factors is vitally important in this sea of competition.

"A corporate identity mantra back in the 1960s was 'make it simple, generic and brown.' If that were really successful, by now the whole world would be that simple. Today, as we create different brands, they are much more complex and have a lot of personality. In the future, I can see a manufacturer having several brands rather than having one big company brand. Even now, it's typical that a manufacturer will have several brands. Even though they have an 80 percent market share, they may have five brands. Nike has gone in that direction. Now they have many different brands that are more specifically geared to individual needs and wants."

Kenneth Botts, Visual Marketing Associates

"As branding evolves, it will become more and more human-like. As humans, we constantly question our understanding of ourselves and our relationship to the world around us. In a similar way, branding will continue to be more introspective. Companies will ask the big questions about how

they take their core beliefs and relate them to their audiences, attracting the kind of consumer relationships that they inevitably want."
Steven Morris, Morris Creative

"There is a heightened need for differentiation. 'Identities—even for major corporations that may have been perceived as being conservative—need to convey approachability. Maybe these firms are looking for a competitive advantage, maybe they're looking for differentiation.'"
Gregory Horn, *Graphic Design USA*, April 2002: "Corporate and Brand Identity: New Challenges, New Competition"

2 Consumer Customization

Technology has allowed for segmentation and customization. Consumers aren't looking for a generalized approach. They want products and services to connect with them on a more personal level, meeting their unique needs. How can this be achieved?

"In the design process for the traditional print world, you now have presses that allow you to create different versions of print. You have been able to personalize addresses in black-and-white type for years now, but with new presses you can actually customize for color imagery. For example, if I'm going to a college and I'm a female vs. a male or I'm studying architecture vs. English, the print materials I receive are different than my neighbors' based on my interests and gender. That's pretty powerful. That's already happening on the web, but it hasn't happened in print until very recently. It will happen in different mediums. It really touches the personality of who is receiving the information. Customizing empowers the designer even more."

Kenneth Botts, Visual Marketing Associates

3 Branding for Niche Markets

Designers are thinking about how to market themselves more effectively as well. A firm can offer niche marketing with regard to consumers, of course, but designers can also think about marketing their own firms within client niches. This can allow designers to become experts within that niche. The more work that is done for a certain client type—music CD cover design, for instance—the more the designer knows about the content, and the more easily they can sell their design services within that niche.

"Once you have established work in a specific sector, it is easy to establish that as a niche, and it positions you up the ladder as a strategic consultant. Now we are developing plans to move into niches that we are interested in working for. Execute that niche, grow that niche and then pick new niches."
P. Michael Zender, Zender + Associates

4 Testing

So is design all about creativity? If it feels good to the designer, it will work in the marketplace? This type of thinking is diminishing. Designers are realizing that they must think more strategically, and that means user testing their work, being more aware of audience responses and being flexible enough to make changes where necessary.

"I think testing will become a much bigger part of design. Of course, the Internet facilitates that and makes it so easy. You can send an e-mail to 300 people and have them look at a new logo design and tell you what they think about it. The results are tabulated automatically with a little survey form. You can make adjustments to your approaches very quickly based on the results you get."
P. Michael Zender, Zender + Associates

"In the future, this type of data tracking may aid in developing a 'value' for each brand. Companies are becoming more interested in trying to put a dollar value on their brands. In some countries they carry the value of the brand on their books.'"
Tom Webb, Monigle Associates

5 Authenticity

With the distrust of business and politics that has grown over the last decade, many companies are moving toward "full disclosure." They realize that, even if they want to, they can't hide their faults and weaknesses behind empty promises. With the Internet comes the power of research, and consumers can easily discover product service flaws before they buy.

"The idea of authenticity and truth is a strong trend in branding. Consumers want something that will connect with them, delivering on its promises. The idea of authenticity and truth is also a growing need for the client. They wish to work

with a team that listens to them and is able to authentically represent their product or service."
Mike Weikert, Iconologic

6 Growing the Brand

There is a need to grow brands, to allow them to evolve and change with the marketplace, building upon past successes and diversifying into new markets. By addressing this client need, designers can strategically position themselves to work with these clients, implementing brand growth and possible brand extensions.

In the article called "Positioning a Brand in the Marketplace," Suzanne Hogan states, "The world is changing so quickly that marketers are constantly challenged to come up with new ways to define and position brands. These trends include:

1   Globalization, a universal homogenization of tastes, emerging market growth and new audiences hungry for products.

2 Demographic shifts and the identification of new classes of consumers with specific needs.

3 Technology, which has spawned new channels of marketing and distribution, such as the Internet and satellite television.

4 Industry consolidation, from insurance to airlines. This results in consumers having fewer brand choices and a greater likelihood that they will become loyal to one brand over others.

5 An increasing emphasis on relationships. Consumers today want brands to be accountable for both their products and their promises. What they really want is the kind of lifetime relationship that existed in the days when buyers and merchants knew each other by name and products were made with care and pride. All of these factors are not only conducive to brand extensions, they necessitate them."

ed in a clean, straightforward way."
John Miller, Partner/Designer, Danilo Black, from
Zender + Associates Z.brochure presentation

"A fallacy with web or interactive design is thinking of people psychographically or demographically. The more relevant issue is what the user's intentions are. What do they want? That falls into two broad categories. One category includes "hunters," and one "shoppers." Shoppers are interested in the experience. They are willing to go in and wander around to explore. Hunters are not interested in experience—they are interested in a piece of data right now."
P. Michael Zender, Zender + Associates

Tim Bedel, author of "The Usability Payoff," offers this process for usability testing, "By integrating early prototyping and usability testing into the design process, the biggest problems can be identified and fixed before it is too late. That is, before the site is released and changes are very expensive, both in terms of development costs and lost business.

"What does it take to do usability testing? Not as much as you may think. It is possible to do effective testing on paper prototypes, which reduces the development costs of building a prototype. It is also possible to concentrate testing on important scenarios within the site (such as the checkout process).

"Most importantly, what it takes is a commitment to the process. Development schedules need to allow for early prototyping and revisions before any real development takes place. Site stakeholders must also commit to going where the testing leads them rather than to making armchair decisions about design."

What can you do to improve the success of your site?

1 If you have an existing site, observe a usability evaluation to see just how difficult it can be for a visitor to conduct business.

2 If you're building a new site, engineer for usability by testing prototypes with real users early and often in the development cycle.

3 Don't let aesthetics alone drive the way your site looks and works.

4 Commit to the idea that your brand is the experience your customers have on the web. People use the web to collect information, compare products and services and gain an understanding of a topic. If your site can support that, it can have an impact on your bottom line.

5 When in doubt, test it.

(www.vianow.com, "The Usability Payoff," Tim Beidel)

9 Digital Marketing

There has been (and likely will continue to be) growth in the area of digital marketing due to speed and cost efficiency. What is digital marketing? Examples include electronic magazines, e-mail newsletters, and opt-in e-mail, where users request (opt) to receive information. (In this case we are not talking about spam, or unwanted junk e-mail.)

An email marketing study in *Opt-in News* noted that "73 percent of worldwide media buyers that have used permission marketing through e-mail believe that it generates better response rates than traditional marketing." Also, "50 percent of media buyers believe e-mail is the most effective vehicle for eliciting marketing responses, followed by 23 percent that favor electronic magazines (e-zines) or e-mail newsletters for their response rates." Zender + Associates, E-direct Marketing

"Direct marketing is an attractive strategy because it offers better targeting, greater personalization, superior measurement capability and efficient use of marketing dollars. E-direct marketing by e-mail allows you to target individuals, receive immediate response, direct individuals to a precise action and measure or 'track' the response."

Zender + Associates, E-direct Marketing

The *Millet to Matisse* Exhibition Z.brochure homepage, above. The quantity and depth of the information and interactivity of this electronic brochure far exceeds a traditional printed promotional brochure.

The *Millet to Matisse* Exhibition Z.brochure secondary pages.

82B

Presentation

"What is a Z.brochure? An electronic brochure that is a stand-alone application, and it does not require separate software to run it. A Z.brochure can offer links to your and other web sites, response e-mail, audio, graphics and photos, embedded surveys (with info going to an online database) and click-through menus to offer inter-activity and enhanced experience.

How do you use a Z.brochure? A Z.brochure is excellent for e-direct marketing, viral marketing, web site downloading, driving traffic to your web site, reducing printing and postage costs, and increasing two-way communication with prospects. A Z.brochure can be distributed as an e-mail attach-ment, CD-ROM, business card CD-ROM, or web site download. Once distributed, the Z.brochure can be detached to the desktop. There, the icon can reside as a 'portal' to your information."

(Zender + Associates)

Z.Digital Premium™ electronic holiday card. The animation progresses from left to right, top to bottom.

"What are Z.Digital Premiums™? Borrowing from the established concept of a direct mail premium or 'special offer' gift, a digital premium is a stand-alone interactive file (that doesn't require separate software) allowing users to click and play a game, regularly view a selected desktop image or interact with an electronic communication that reinforces your brand, product, company or organization. Digital premiums are tools that aid in driving traffic to your web site. We can create interactive games, custom screensavers with web links, desktop images or electronic greeting cards. Digital premiums are unique, cost effective, reflect a level of sophistication and, most importantly, users can forward the electronic file to friends and associates, repeating brand exposure. They are distributed as an e-mail attachment or as a direct URL web link for download."

(Zender + Associates)

Celebrate Life

CATCH A SNOWFLAKE
MAKE SOMECOLOR

Celebrate Life
now & in the new year

Z.Digital Premium electronic holiday card. Animation progresses from left to right.

Design

10 Design Awareness

The awareness of design is growing in the United States. The success of Target stores is a great example of how "design for the masses" can work. Design is not only for the elite, it is for everyone. Design is about communication, and positive and effective communication is important to everyone. More businesses are beginning to understand how design can help to differentiate them from the competition and aid them in communicating their messages to their constituencies. "I think business in general is headed towards a little bit of what Europe went through years ago, and it's becoming more design aware. Businesses will always have products, services, ideas and concepts that need to be communicated to their audiences," says Fred Warren, Tank Design. So as technology, and the way we get the message across, changes and escalates, the need will remain the same. Designers must learn to be flexible about how they communicate that message and be ready to turn on a dime when a new form of communication—or a variation on an old form—becomes familiar to the marketplace.

11 E-mail Consulting

Technology has transformed the way designers produce projects, and it is transforming the way designers communicate their work to clients. More and more, e-mail is coming into play and aiding professionals in conferring about design process and approving design solutions.

"More and more we are doing e-mail consulting. We have established relationships with many of our clients, so this is an efficient way of working. We are doing a project in Spain, for example, and we've only been there once. Since then, communication has been accomplished through weekly teleconferences. The night before the teleconference, we send PDF files of everything to the client.

We also build and send models for our three-dimensional projects. Because of e-mail and technology, we can communicate faster, and this has made work a lot easier. You can leave voice mail. You can send e-mail. You can get your answers a lot more quickly and include a lot more people in the process. We like the way it's very straightforward and simple. It gets the job done. "

Kiku Obata, Kiku Obata & Company

12 The Business of Design

Design is still about aesthetics, but it has also become more about business. In the design programs of the 1980s, few students learned anything about business practice or strategy. Today, many programs have already incorporated, or are moving toward incorporating, business knowledge into their programs.

"It's all about doing business. The future will be about understanding the world economics, the world cultures and the markets and how to sell to them. Those are traditional business practices that you need knowledge of."
Dave Mason, SamataMason

"Design is also moving in a more entrepreneurial direction, more proactive and less reactionary. For instance, a designer may think, 'I think I want to work with these five or six clients and I'm going to make it my business for them to get to know me and for me to get to know them. I have a dialogue and a relationship with them, even though there's not a specific project, so that when a project comes along, I can offer them more strategic, proactive thinking, not just react to the problem at hand.'"
Ken Carbone, Carbone Smolan Agency

A

Above the fold

The portion of the web page that is visible to the user without scrolling the page. The area above the fold is the most prominent location for content.

Ad banner

An advertisement on a web page that links to another web site and is often placed at the top of the page in the shape of a banner. There are actually many shapes and sizes set by the Internet Advertising Bureau (IAB). Some are even rather small and are called buttons.

Full banner: 468 x 60 pixels

Full banner/vertical navigation bar: 392 x 72 pixels

Half banner: 234 x 60 pixels

Vertical banner: 120 x 240 pixels

Button 1: 120 x 90 pixels

Button 2: 120 x 60 pixels

Square button: 125 x 125 pixels

Micro button: 88 x 31 pixels

Ad rotation

The rotation of ad spaces can be accomplished automatically by software at a central site/server.

Ad space

A portion of a web page reserved exclusively for advertisements.

Affiliate marketing

When one web site sells or promotes the products and services of another site, called an affiliate.

Address

The location, expressed as a string of letters and/or numbers, of an internet server (IP address), an e-mail user or a specific file or web page.

Analog

Refers to the electronic transmission of signals of varying frequency or amplitude to carrier waves of a given frequency of alternating electromagnetic current. Phone and broadcast transmission are examples. A modem converts the computer's

93B

digital information to the phone line's analog signal, and vice versa.

Antidisintermediation

Internet consumers have direct access to goods and services previously requiring an intermediary. E-businesses are able to sell goods more efficiently and at lower prices by cutting out the middleman (travel agent, retailer, etc.)

B

B2B

Business-to-business. Refers to businesses selling traditionally or through a web site to other businesses (wholesalers).

B2C

Business-to-consumer. Refers to selling goods directly to the consumer. Addresses the business and marketing strategies of promoting and selling on- or off-line.

B2E

Business-to-employee. The focus of the business is not the consumer or other businesses but the employee, specifically in attracting and retaining qualified staff.

Bandwidth test

A program that sends a file of a particular size over a network to another computer, measuring the time it takes the file to reach its destination. The results can vary widely because there are many factors that influence the speed of download time.

Below the fold

The content on a web page that isn't visible without scrolling down. This location isn't considered as valuable as that above the fold because it is not as readily visible.

Benchmark

A standard of measurement to test performance, in this case, of competing hardware or software products.

Beyond the banner

Refers to the ways, beyond banners ads, to advertise on the web.

Bolt-on

Used to describe products or systems added on to a web site. Most commonly used for adding an e-commerce solution to an existing web site—an online store, for instance.

Bookmark

A saved link to a web page added to a list of saved links, usually located in the menu bar. Some sites have "bookmark buttons," which prompt the user to save the page as a bookmark for future use.

Browser

An application program that allows users to access and interact with the Internet. Examples are Netscape Navigator and Microsoft Internet Explorer.

Buffer page

An additional page located "between" the ad banner and the web site used to advertise a special offer or highlight specific information before going to the main web site.

C

CPM

Cost per thousand (M). A web marketing term referring to the amount of money associated with a particular number of web page views.

Click-and-mortar

A brick-and-mortar company that establishes an online presence, maintaining both sales outlets.

Click here

A "click here" button is an often overused strategy to persuade the viewer to click on the link to go to another web page.

Clickstream

A recorded number of pages a user accesses in moving through a web site. This information can help web designers and owners to understand more clearly how viewers use and interact with their pages.

Click rate

The percentage of ad views that results in the user actually interacting with/clicking on an ad banner.

Contextual commerce

Editorial content that is used to help sell products online by blurring the edges between objective and editorial information about the product or service.

Cookie

Information that a web site puts on a hard drive or

server so it can recall facts about the user. Specifically it records preferences and tracks Internet activities.

Counter

A program that counts—and normally displays—the number of visitors to a web site, demonstrating its popularity.

Cybrarian

An online researcher performing information retrieval on the Internet.

Cyberspace

The digital world, originally coined by William Gibson in his novel *Neuromancer*.

D

DSL

Digital Subscriber Line. A technology for delivering high bandwidth to homes and businesses using copper telephone lines. These lines can carry data and voice signals.

Digital

Electronic technology that generates, stores and processes data in positive and nonpositive terms, expressed in a string of 1s (positive) and 0s (non-positive).

Domain name

The address or URL of a specific web site, locating a particular organization or company on the Internet. Along with the suffixes previously used in domain names on the web (.com, .net, .edu, .org), now there are new ones. They include .arts for arts and cultural entities, .firm for business, .info for information services, .non for individuals, .rec for recreation and entertainment, .store for merchants and .web for web services.

Dotcom

Any web site intended for use by business. The name is based on the ".com" portion of the domain name. This term became associated with the failure of many Internet businesses during the late 1990s.

Downloading

Refers to the transmission of a file from one computer to another. For the Internet user, to "download a file" means to request it from another computer or web site and then receive it.

Drop-down menu

Appears by clicking on the down arrow on the side of a select box. The menu, or list of options, drops down to allow the user access to choices.

E

E2E

Exchange-to-exchange. This form of B2B is the exchange of information between web sites that are themselves exchanging information, goods or services between businesses.

E-business

Electronic business. The actions of business on the Internet, whether selling, servicing, buying, collaborating or communicating.

E-commerce

Electronic commerce. Conducting business online. Buying, selling and servicing on the Internet.

E-form

Electronic form. An electronic version of a paper form used for electronic submission.

E-mail

Electronic mail. The exchange of written messages from one computer to another. E-mail can be distributed to an individual or a group of people.

E-paper

Electronic paper. Portable, reusable display and storage device that looks like paper but can be repeatedly refreshed electronically. Use mostly for electronic books, newspapers, signs, and displays.

Emoticon

Sometimes referred to as a "smiley." A short sequence of keystrokes usually resembling a facial expression. Used mostly in e-mail and chatting.

:-)   Smile

;-)   Smile with a wink

:<})	User with mustache, smiling	=:O	Frightened
:-||	Mad	=8O	Bug-eyed with fright
:-(	Sad	:-}	Embarrassed smile
:`-(	Crying	;-^)	Tongue in cheek
:-))	Really happy	8:-)	Glasses on forehead
:-D	Big grin	8:[	Gorilla
:-*	Kiss	0:-)	Angel
:-o	Surprise	]:-|[	Robot
:-|	Grim	(:V)	Duck
:-P	Sticking out your tongue	3:-o	Cow
:-/	Perplexed	And there are many others!	

E-tailing

A form of e-commerce where businesses, many of which have no brick-and-mortar counterpart, leverage the Internet to sell products.

Extranet

A private network that uses the Internet to securely share business information with vendors, suppliers or partners. It can be thought of as part of a company's intranet extended to a select group outside the company.

F

File transfer

Movement of one or more files from one computer to another using an electronic storage medium like a disk or CD, over a network, or using the Internet and file transfer protocol (FTP).

Frames

Independently controlled sections of a web page used in creating a web site. Each section is built as a separate HTML file with a master file that identifies each section of the page when requested.

G

GIF

Graphics Interchange Format. Image file format for use on the web that is usually used for high-contrast images and line art.

GIF animation (animated GIF)

A type of GIF format that shows a series of images one after another, or on top of one another, at a specific speed to imply animated movement.

GUI

Graphical User Interface. Allows interaction with the computer. The most familiar GUIs are the MacIntosh or Windows operating systems and their applications.

H

HCI

Human Computer Interaction. The study of how people interact with computers. Many factors must be taken into consideration, including cultural influences and learning styles.

HTML

HyperText Markup Language. The set of markup symbols or codes inserted in a file for viewing on a World Wide Web browser. The code tells the browser how to display the web page's text and images. Each individual markup code is referred to as a "tag" or "element."

Hit

Accessing a file and its elements. Every element (images or text) on a web page counts as one hit. Actual page requests are a more accurate way of determining the popularity of a web site.

Homepage

The front, or "welcome" page of a web site that serves as a starting point for navigation through the site and an introduction to the site's content.

Host

A web server that stores and serves the pages for one or more web sites.

Hypermedia

Extends the idea of a hypertext link to include links for sound, video and virtual reality. Also implies a higher level of interactivity than that of hypertext.

Hypertext

Organization and connection of information into links the user can choose. This was the main concept that led to the World Wide Web—a lot of information connected by a huge number of hypertext links.

Hub

A common connector point for devices in a network.

I

IP address

A number that identifies each sender or receiver of information over the Internet.

ISP

Internet Service Provider. A company that provides access to the Internet by establishing an account with the user.

Impressions

The number of times an ad banner is downloaded and seen by users. Impressions are how most web ads are sold, and the cost is quoted in terms of CPM impressions.

IO

Insertion Order. A formal order to run an ad campaign identifying the campaign name, the web site receiving the order, the buyer, ads to be run, ad sizes, beginning and end dates, the CPM, total cost and other billing information.

Incubator

An organization of services created to nurture young businesses and business ideas. Internet business incubators create, launch and operate Internet businesses using a network of investors.

Instant messaging

A way to see if someone is connected to the Internet and if they are, to exchange messages with them via instant message delivery. This differs from e-mail, which has a time delay.

Interactive/Interactivity

The dialog that occurs between a computer program and a user.

Internet

A worldwide system of computers and computer networks in which users can access information and communicate with other users.

Internet time

The concept that events occur faster on the Internet, or that the Internet is affecting the general perception of the pace of time.

Internet traffic

Statistics on the speed and quality of data transfer, frequently posted by several large companies on the web.

Intranet

A private, limited access network used to share company information and resources among employees.

Inventory

The number of ad views a web site must sell over a given period of time, usually figured by the month.

J

JPEG

Joint Photographic Experts Group. One of the most frequently used image file types on the World Wide Web. Works well for photographs and full-color images. Named after the original committee that wrote this standard for image compression.

JPEG optimizer

Used for making file sizes smaller so they can be downloaded more quickly.

K

Keyword

The word(s) a user types into a search box to begin an online search.

L

Link

Text or image area that a user clicks to connect to or reference another file, document or page.

111B

M

M-payment

Mobile payment. A point-of-sale payment transferred through a mobile device, such as a cellular phone or personal digital assistant (PDA).

Meta tag

An HTML tag that points out specific information about a particular web document, controlling how the web page is indexed by search engines. This affects how the page will come up as a choice in the user's search.

Modem

Hardware that modulates outgoing digital signals from a computer, converts them to analog signals for transfer over conventional telephone lines, and demodulates incoming analog signals and converts them to digital.

Morphing

The transformation of one image into another image through a series of small steps, implying motion.

N

Navigation Bar

Directional tools often placed in a row or bar to help guide the user through the maze of pages in a web site. The sections of the web site are listed and linked so users can navigate their way. Also called a "nav bar."

O

121

One-to-one. A marketing strategy in which each customer is treated as a special, unique individual, as opposed to part of the group of similar people.

OSP

Online Service Provider. A company that provides customer-only content to subscribers. Many also offer Internet access. An example of such a service is America Online (AOL).

Online

Being connected to the Internet. Can also be used to describe the variety of activities of users: chatting, shopping, searching, etc.

Opt-in e-mail

A message containing information that a user requests to receive by e-mail.

P

Page

Each page of a web site is an individual HTML file with its own web address.

Page request or page views

The number of requests for a web page from a server. This is the preferred way to estimate traffic as opposed to using "hits."

Personalization

Tailoring pages to individual users' characteristics and preferences, is a version of one-to-one (121) marketing. The goal is to meet the customer's needs more effectively and efficiently in hopes of improving sells and repeat visits to the site.

Portal

Web sites that serve as access points to other locations on the web. They commonly providing services such as e-mail, chat rooms, shopping, searching, etc. Yahoo is a good example of a portal.

Presence

Web presence is another term for a web site. It seems to imply that the site is an experience and is not tied to a specific location but is somewhere in cyberspace.

S

Search engine

A "card catalog" for the Internet, the search engine will index and search for information using keywords specified by the user.

Select box

A space-saving device on a web page that, when clicked on, shows the user a variety of different options and allows them to choose either one or multiple selections. A drop-down menu is an example of a select box.

Server

A host computer, or computer program, on a network that stores information. When a user requests specific information, the server transfers it across the network to the user's computer.

Shopping cart

A common metaphor for web pages where a

consumer's selections are shown before final purchase through a checkout page. The user reads and makes choices and purchases of online products or services from the shopping cart. Also referred to as a "basket" or a "shopping bag."

Site

A web site is a collection of files beginning with an entry file/page. From this home page the user can navigate through the other pages in the site.

Site map

An overview of a web site's content and organization. It can be in a list/outline form or in a graphical chart form. Many site map entries also act as links to various portions of the site.

Sitelet

A small section of a web site that has a specific function or purpose. Sometimes users are encouraged to go to a sitelet directly without going to the main site. Also referred to as a "mini-site."

Snail mail

Slang term for the regular postal service. Refers to the time it takes to receive traditional mail (as slow as a snail), vs. the speed of e-mail.

Solution

This word has been recently attached to many computer terms, such as "small business database solution." Refers to the fact that this product or service will answer all the consumer's problems.

Spam

Refers to unsolicited e-mail on the Internet. The electronic form of bulk mail or junk mail (depending on your perspective).

Splash page

An introduction page or animated (Flash) presentation before the home page of a site. Serves to build excitement and interest about the site and its content but does not normally contain much content on its own.

Standard

An acknowledged or "agreed upon" basis for comparing or measuring something. This term is often used in the computer industry as a group of specifications with which companies can develop products that are compatible with one another.

Start-up

A business that is just getting started.

Style guide

A set of guidelines, usually in the form of a manual, to insure consistency in formatting and developing a web site or any print material. Style guides normally contain standards for design choices, such as fonts, colors, photography style and overall look and feel. They can also contain more technical information, such as HTML formatting.

Style sheet

Borrowed from print publishing, this term refers to the definition of a document's appearance (including typography, page formatting, color, etc.) and is typically specified electronically to achieve consistency throughout pages.

T

Tag

A command or instruction in HTML code.

Top-level domain

The most general part of the domain name. For instance, it may be "edu" for education or "fr" for France.

Turnkey

A complete system that has everything needed and ready to operate.

U

URL

Uniform Resource Locator. The address of a file on

the Internet, containing the protocol name (http), the domain name (www.myname.com) identifying the specific computer the file is housed on and a hierarchical description of the file location on that computer (www.myname.com/pegpage).

Usability

The level at which a product (software, web site) meets a user's needs and goals.

User testing

Testing a product with potential users in the product's specific target market to gain insights into their interaction with a product prototype. Commonly, user testing results in improvements to the final product.

V

VC money

Venture capital money. Funding from investors at the early stages of the development of risk-oriented business ventures.

Vertical portal

Portals that are industry specific and cater to a narrower target audience than a broad-based portal.

W

Wallet

A small software program used for online purchase transactions.

Web developer

A person who builds and programs web site architecture. Not to be confused with a web designer.

Web page

Each page of a web site is an individual HTML file with its own web address. Also referred to simply as a page.

Web server

A host computer, or computer program, on a network that stores information. When a user requests specific information, the server transfers it across the network to the user's computer. Also referred to as a server.

Web site

A web site is a collection of files beginning with an entry file/page. From this home page the user can navigate through the other pages in the web site. Also referred to as a site.

Webmaster

The person who is ultimately responsible for the maintenance of a web site, including the functionality and updating of content.

Welcome page

The introductory page in a web site, also referred to as the home page.

WWW

World Wide Web. A global hypertext system that a user can navigate by clicking hyperlinks, which take the user to another document with hyperlinks, and so on and so on. These documents can be housed on web servers anywhere in the world.

Sources: www.netlingo.com, www.whatis.com

B

Brand associations

A consumer's associations with a particular brand.

Brand audit

An analysis of all aspects of a company's brand. Usually performed when revitalizing a brand.

Brand awareness

The relative recognition of a brand in the minds of consumers.

Branded environment

The application of the brand identity in the three-dimensional environment through signage, for example.

Brand equity

The value of the brand, developed over a period of time, and its related power to influence consumers' purchase decisions and their perception of the brand.

Brand essence

The core value(s) of the brand.

Brand extension

Building on the equity of an existing brand by creating a new, related product or service.

Brand identity

A unique set of visual elements that identify a company or organization, communicating the core message of the brand.

Brand identity manual

A plan, in the form of a printed, CD or online manual, for the use and implementation of the company's visual assets, including the logo, typography, color palette, additional graphic elements, page formats, writing style and brand voice.

Brand image

The image or perception of the brand in the eyes of the consumer, developed through experience with the brand.

Brand loyalty

The "measure" of the loyalty of a consumer to a particular brand.

Brand manager

The "overseer" of the brand.

Brand personality

Defining and describing a brand using human characteristics and personality traits.

Brand positioning

Specifically identifying for the consumer the company's points of difference and benefits to differentiate the company from the competition.

Brand promise

The expression to the consumer of a company's relevant and authentic benefits and beliefs.

Brand revitalization

The process of recreating a brand identity beginning with renaming (sometimes the previous name is retained) and positioning, progressing through to execution and implementation of all visual elements. Also called rebranding.

Brand strategy

A long-term plan for the implementation and communication of the brand to the target audience.

Brand value proposition

A listing of the benefits and values of the brand, especially those things that connect with the consumer and help to build a relationship with them.

C

Co-branding

Two or more brands in cooperation, making a joint offer to consumers.

Communications audit

An analysis of a company's internal and external communications (visual and verbal).

Communications plan

A company's goals and objectives for communications and the methods for implementing and achieving them.

Corporate identity

The visual components that identify a company (logo, stationery, packaging, etc.)

D

Demographics

Information about the size or characteristics of a target audience. For instance, their gender, age, income and education levels.

I

Image attributes

The elements that differentiate the tone, personality and style of a company from others like it.

Image criteria

The definition of the desired brand personality, which aids in the process of creating the brand.

Interactive branding

Implementation of the brand identity through web and interactive design applications.

Integrated communication

Creating communications that deliver a coordinated and holistic message across media.

Integrated branding

A strategy to integrate all actions and messages within a company or organization and externally to their audience.

L

Logo

A group of letters (logotype) or image (mark or symbol) that represent a company or organization to its audience.

M

Mission statement

Defines the goals, objectives and values of a company and serves to unite employees.

N

Naming

The strategic process of carefully choosing the most appropriate name for an organization or company.

Nomenclature system

Developing a family of names that are related to or associated with a parent company.

P

Perception gap

When the brand's assets have not been effectively communicated to the brand's audience.

Permission marketing

Developing a relationship and partnership with the target audience through appropriate market research and the development of specific messages to segmented audiences. This approach results in the target audience inviting the relationship with the brand.

Performance gap

When a brand's assets are out of step with the offerings of competitors in the marketplace.

Positioning statement

A statement that describes a company and what they do, differentiates them from the competition and outlines the benefits to the consumer.

Psychographics

Information about a target audience that focuses on their interests, perceptions and values, as opposed to their demographics (age or gender, for instance).

S

Sub-brand

A product or service that is a smaller part of the larger parent brand but has its own identity and brand recognition.

Service brand

A brand that represents a service or group of services.

U

User personality

Defining the typical consumer of the product or service by specific personality traits. This helps to get "inside the head" of the consumer.

Sources:

www.stamats.com/applications/stories/
    branding.asp

www.get-serious.com/busdev/branding-
    glossary.html

www.lippincottmercer.com/publications/s95_
    glossary.html

www.whatis.com: searchEBusiness.techtarget.
    com/sDefinition/0,,sid19_gci211535,00.html

www.landor.com

300FeetOut

Nina Dietzel, Co-founder

292 Ivy Street, Suite A

San Francisco, CA 94102

P: 415.551.2377, F: 415.551.2385

www.300feetout.com

Carbone Smolan Agency

Ken Carbone, Principal

22 West 19th Street, 10th Floor

New York, NY 10011

P: 212.807.0011, F: 212.807.0870

www.carbonesmolan.com

Iconologic

Mike Weikert, Creative Director

40 Inwood Circle

Atlanta, GA 30309

P: 404.260.4500, F: 404.260.4581

www.iconologic.com

Kiku Obata

Kiku Obata, President

6161 Delmar Boulevard, Suite 200

St. Louis, MO 63112

P: 314.361.3110, F: 314.361.4716

www.kikuobata.com

Landor Associates

Phil Duncan, Managing Director

110 Shillito Place

Cincinnati, OH 45202

P: 513.419.2300, F: 513.221.3532

www.landor.com

Leonhardt:Fitch

Sue Nixon, CEO

1218 Third Avenue, Suite 620

Seattle, WA 98101

P: 206.624.0551, F: 206.624.0875

www.leonhardt-fitch.com

Monigle Associates

Tom Webb, Principal–Graphic Design

150 Adams Street

Denver, CO 80206

P: 303.388.9358, F: 303.321.7939

www.monigle.com

Morris Creative

Steve Morris, Head Honcho

660 Ninth Avenue, Studio 3

San Diego, CA 92101

P: 619.234.1211, F: 877.234.1210

www.thinkfeelwork.com

137B

SamataMason

Greg Samata, Principal/Designer

101 South First Street

West Dundee, IL 60118

P: 847.428.8600, F: 847.428.6564

www.samatamason.com

Tank Design

Scott Watts, Partner

158 Sidney Street

Cambridge, MA 02139

P: 617.995.4000, F: 617.995.4001

www.tankdesign.com

The VIA Group
David Bull, Director, Strategic Branding and Design
330 West Spring Street, Suite 400
Columbus, OH 43215
P: 614.628.8170, F: 614.628.8177
www.vianow.com

VSA Partners
Jamie Koval, Partner
1347 S. State Street
Chicago, IL 60605
P: 312.895.5090, F: 312.895.5720
www.vsapartners.com

Visual Marketing Associates

Ken Botts, Principal

Firefly Building

123 Webster Street, Studio 3

Dayton, OH 45402

P: 937.223.7500, F: 937.223.6800

www.vmai.com

Wolff Olins

Robbie Laughton, Creative Director

10 Regents Wharf, All Saints Street

London , N1 9RL, United Kingdom

P: 44 (0) 20 7713 7733, F: 44 (0) 20 7713 0217

www.wolff-olins.com

Zender + Associates

P. Michael Zender, Principal

2311 Park Avenue

Cincinnati, OH 45206

P: 513.961.1790, F: 513.961.1799

www.zender.com

141B

Bibliography

Magazines:

Graphic Design USA, April 2002, "Corporate and Brand Identity: New Challenges, New Competition," pgs. 51–59.

Interviews, promotional materials and web sites from the following design firms:

Tank Design
The VIA Group
Kiku Obata
Wolff Olins
Carbone Smolan Agency
Morris Creative
Iconologic
Monigle Associates
Landor Associates
Zender + Associates
300FeetOut
VSA Partners
Leonhardt:Fitch
Visual Marketing Associates
SamataMason

White papers on the following web sites:

www.lippincottmercer.com

   Creating the Preeminent Global Brand: Building Powerful Strategies that Strengthen Brand Equity,

Kenneth J. Roberts

Orchestrating a Successful Brand Identity: Creating Harmony Instead of Cacophony

Positioning a Brand in the Marketplace, Suzanne Hogan

Speed, Content and Navigation: The Winning Trifecta of an Effective Web Site

Who?.com The Race to Build Internet Brands, Richard H. Wilke

Rethinking Brand Strategy: A "Mindshare" Manifesto, Eric Almquist and Kenneth J. Roberts

Glossary of Identity Terms

www.vianow.com

Multidimensional Brand Experience, Rich Rico

Multidimensional Branding for the 21st Century, Rich Rico

The Usability Payoff, Tim Beidel

Building Brands on Wall Street, Rich Rico

Sincerity Marketing: Delivering the Right Message, to the Right Customer, at the Right Time, Christopher Seid

Is Paper the Most Advanced Communications Medium?

143B

www.wolff-olins.com

After the Stampede: Three Winning Strategies for Internet Success, Angela Andal Ancion (published in *Market Leader*, Spring 2002)

Why Brand-Building Belongs in the Boardroom, John Williamson (published in *Sunday Express*, June 9, 2002)

The Lie Detectors, Richard Gold (published in *Blueprint Magazine*, September 2001)

The Power of Love Brands, Christoph Santner (published in *Die Welt*, November 2001)

Using Brand to Escape the National Straightjacket, John Williamson (published in *Economic Times, Brand Equity*, June 2001)

Beyond Brand: The Big Idea, Robert Jones (published in *Management Journal*, October 2001)

Brand Matters, John Williamson (published in *Real Deals*, December 2001)

www.landor.com

Do's and Don'ts: Tips for Creating and Sustaining Breakaway Brands™ in the New Economy

My Son Adolf: Why Naming a Brand is Like Naming a Child

Wielding a Brand Name: The Underutilized

*Weapon for Competing in a Crowded Marketplace?
Branding*, Hayes Roth

*A Paradigm for Brand Pruning: The Answer May
Be In the Sky*, Allen Adamson

*The Future of Branding Based on Current Trends:
You Say You Want an Evolution...*, Allen Adamson

*Brand Architecture Trends: A Look at Key Issues
and Emerging Solutions*, Allen Adamson

A New Era for Corporate Identity

360 Degrees: Holistic Corporate Communications

Branding Dictionary

www.monigle.com

The Core of Integration Is the Brand, Don E.
Schultz (published in *Marketing Management*,
Spring 2001)

www.iamawiz.com/branding

Brand Building: What's in a Name?, John
Freivalds

E-Branding

Percepts of Branding

Brands—The Key to the Future

Branding on the Net

www.thinkfeelwork.com

Truth About Designer-Client Relationships, Steven Morris

Redefining "Good Work." Why Design Really Matters, Steven Morris

The Power of Emotion in Visual Communication, Steven Morris

www.netlingo.com

www.stamats.com

Branding Glossary, Fritz McDonald

www.get-serious.com

A Glossary of Branding Terminology, Jaffe Associates, Inc.

www.brand.com

A Short Introduction To Branding, BrandSolutions, 2000

www.all-biz.com

Just What is a "Brand"?, Hollis Thomases

www.whatis.techtarget.com

www.sojoinc.com

Branding Dictionary

www.dictionary.com

www.emarketer.com

Books:

A New Brand World: Eight Principles for Achieving Brand Leadership in the 21st Century. Scott Bedbury and Stephen Fenichell, Viking Press, 2002.

Branding Across Borders: A Guide to Global Brand Marketing. James R. Gregory and Jack G. Wiechmann (contributor), McGraw-Hill Trade, 2001.

Branding Online. Keith Drew, Universe Books, 2002.

Design for Interaction: User-Friendly Graphics. Lisa Baggerman, Rockport Publishers, Gloucester, Massachusetts, 2000.

Designer's Guide to Marketing: Painless Principles for Creating Design That Sells. Betsy Newberry, North Light Books, Cincinnati, Ohio, 1997.

Designing Brands: Market Success Through Graphic Distinction. Emily Schrubbe-Potts, Rockport Publishers, Gloucester, Massachusetts, 2000.

Designing Business: Multiple Media, Multiple Disciplines. Clement Mok, Adobe Press, San Jose, California, 1996.

Designing Corporate Identity: Graphic Design as a Business Strategy. Pat Matson Knapp, Rockport Publishers, Gloucester, Massachusetts, 2001.

Designing Web Usability. Jakob Nielsen, New Riders Publishing, Indianapolis, Indiana, 2000.

Digital Portfolio: 26 Design Portfolios Unzipped. Anne T. McKenna, Rockport Publishers, Gloucester, Massachusetts, 2000.

Homepage Usability: 50 Websites Deconstructed. Jakob Nielsen and Marie Tahir, New Riders Publishing, Indianapolis, Indiana, 2002.

Logos: Logo, Identity, Brand, Culture. Conway Lloyd Morgan, Rotovision, East Sussex, England, 1999.

Marks of Excellence: The History and Taxonomy of Trademarks. Per Mollerup, Phaidon Press, London, England, 1997.

The 22 Immutable Laws of Branding. Al Ries and Laura Ries, Harper Collins, 2002.

The Digital Designer: The Graphic Artist's Guide to the New Media. Steven Heller and Daniel Drennan, Watson-Guptill Publications, New York, New York, 1997.

Type in Motion: Innovations in Digital Graphics. Jeff Bellantoni and Matt Woolman, Rizzoli, New York, New York, 1999.

What is Branding: Graphic Design Handbook. Piers Schmidt, Rotovision, 2003.

Permissions

150B

Index